MW01678665

Avoiding Potholes, *Speed* Bumps, & Long Dusty Roads

Avoiding Potholes, *Speed* Bumps, & Long Dusty Roads

A Workbook for Healthy Relationships

Wayne Marsonette
with foreward by
Gail Russell

Manufactured in the United States of America

Husky/Bang Printing, Brainard, MN, Book Printers Network

ISBN: 0-9654885-0-0

Marsonette, Wayne W.

Avoiding Potholes, Speed Bumps, & Long Dusty Roads: a males view of relationships and healthy dating: with foreward by Gail Russell.

Cover design: Wayne Marsonette

Setup and typography: Le Graphics
(541) 767-0720

Publisher: GeminImage Publishing

PO Box 70712

Eugene, Or 97401

FAX (541) 744-7122

For my daughters, Susan and Kelly.

Table of Contents

Foreword

I have known Wayne for over a decade. Our children went to school together, and we were co-workers in our "other life." We are partners, friends and "co-conspirators" in editing this work, to produce a practical and enjoyable guide through the maze of dating.

For Wayne, this is a subject of timely relevance, since finding himself as a mid-life single. If you are exploring singleness for the first time, or if you have reentered the dating arena, there is something in this workbook to benefit you on your journey.

Wayne is not a counselor, professional therapist, or psychologist, but he is an introspective and critical thinker who has learned something about this business and yearns to share his experiences. It is his hope that this will result in the development of healthy relationships in your life.

For me, this has been an enjoyable learning experience, as well. I've had to learn to be both a better listener and communicator. May you gain as much as we did.

Gail Russell

Preface

The title of this work was chosen to engage your thinking in a new way. When referenced to dating, the terms go a long way to describe some of the common pitfalls and saboteurs of success. If you are willing to commit yourself to some hard work, this book could change the bottom line in your relationships. Your commitment and perseverance will determine your success.

This is a study of one male's view of dating and how to create healthy relationships. This book includes a workbook to engage your mind, and challenge your thinking. Use of this tool will make you an active participant in handling many difficult situations.

Dating, like climbing a mountain requires a plan. To proceed without one, is to court disaster. The endeavor is destined to fail. You must have an understanding of what you are trying to accomplish. If you have ever had a failed relationship, this primer is for you. There are some everyday skills dating singles should be able to develop after they understand a few concepts and have set some definite guidelines and goals. This book is designed to give you the tools to make your plan work.

This book is intended to take you step by step through the planning stages of your dating adventures. There are explicit directions on defining your wants, the preparation of the date and the excitement of being in a relationship.

The most important classrooms for this text are in the relationships that develop.

The following is a series of questions and convictions that I have found to be useful. I use them to define what I seek in a person with whom I'll spend time. I believe these ideas, when implemented, can lead to meaningful and healthy relationships. This is my criteria and my opinion. I am not passing moral judgment. My intent is to share my experience. Use some of the ideas. Your success may please you.

This book, of creative ideas and basic knowledge, is written for singles who are interested in doing better the next time around.

Acknowledgments

Many thanks to all of the people who made this book possible. The idea of something written was first conceived in the fall of 1994. This publication was brought about after many hours of discussion with Hollie Kitman, Debbie Mikilas, Sandy Lemmon, and Gail Russell.

The title is a gift of Gail Russell. I liked it when I first heard it. Then, the darn thing just grew on me.

I wish to thank my former spouse, Marcia. I learned a lot in our twenty-year marriage. Many of the experiences were positive.

The women that I have known and dated have all lent themselves to a part of this. What a great learning experience for me.

My mother is not responsible for my behavior. She did a wonderful job raising me. Too bad some of the lessons came the hard way.

Guidance was given, in times of trouble, by Mark Norwicki.

Lynden Duke was the educator who introduced me to the concept of the correct use of our language. He was the one who directed me to look at the misuse of moral judgments and how to define when feelings and ideas were to be appropriately used.

Thank you, all.

"Advice To Young Men And
(incidentally) To Young Women
In The Middle And Higher
Ranks Of Life," 1829

"It is the duty, and ought to be the pleasure, of age and experience to warn and instruct youth and to come to the aid of experience. When sailors have discovered rocks or breakers, and have had the good luck to escape with life from amidst them, they, unless they be pirates or barbarians as well as sailors, point out the spots for the placing of buoys and of lights, in order that others may not be exposed to the danger which they have so narrowly escaped. What man of common humanity, having, by good luck, missed being engulfed in a quagmire or quicksand, will withhold from his neighbors a knowledge of the peril without which the dangerous spots are not to be approached?"

William Cobbett

Potholes

You've been moving along, blissfully ignorant of cues and warning signs. All of a sudden, you sense a "bottoming out," and a violent jarring. First reaction: shock, followed quickly by a sense of panic. Did I sustain damage? Are the shocks shot? Where did that come from? Why wasn't I forewarned? Welcome to a relationship "pothole.

Speed Bumps

You're cruising... your relationship seems to be moving forward nicely, and you figure that to pick up a bit of speed wouldn't be harmful. Slow down! In this context, a speed bump is an indicator of manic excitement. Do you or your partner require constant activity and mania to enjoy your times together? Be forewarned. This makes for a real roller-coaster ride.

Long Dusty Roads

Long Dusty Roads is evidenced by the joyless journey. If you've stayed in a dry and dying relationship too long, you've no doubt stayed because you believe that eventually you may realize your goal. Consider, first, when your "goal" is worth the joyless journey. (This is not meant to be an "escape" clause). A few difficulties experienced in a relationship are normal and healthy. We are speaking here of an obviously untenable situation.

Chapter 1

Defining My Terms

Healthy Dating

Healthy: whole or sound. Dating: keeping an appointment or engagement.

Face value

The term in common usage is *honesty*. *Face value* gets me more mileage. Honesty is an inflammatory word with moral encumbrances. Face value says that the statement or action is without deceit.

Each develops, over the course of our lives, a "moral code." This encompasses our perceptions of what is or is not acceptable. If a person can be taken at face value, that person has a "moral code" that is operational; their actions are in keeping with their code. This person then operates with integrity. Even if I disagree with their "code," the fact that they operate in integrity allows me to take them at face value.

Team-based relationship

The team concept is designed for people to define and do a job with an end product. This works very well in many businesses. I suggest that it can also work in a personal relationship. Sometimes a job can be a joy and sometimes it can be a trial. Some days are easier than others. When there is a team approach, one person is not stuck with the housework, or with fixing the car. There is no master who decides what the other will do. All parties agree to do the job, and stay with it until the end product is achieved.

Sovereign-based relationship

When this country was settled, the men were told, "Go to America. Be your own king. Your home will be your castle; your children and wives your subjects. You are the sovereign."

The problem with a sovereign is that they believe they rule by divine right; therefore, no one may question their decisions. This was a society based on control and dominance.

Attitudes are hard-dying. For many, dictatorial mannerisms prevail. Our forefathers grew up in this atmosphere of dictatorial relationships. No wonder that the influence has carried over into our lives.

Because of these attitudes, we hear these kinds of statements: "My life is my own," "I have a right to…," "I give compliments," "That's your job," "You have to do it my way," "I let you," "I am entitled to…," "I expect my dinner on time," "You can get some tonight," "He won't let me," "Look at what I have done for you." These expressions are birthed in the Sovereign/Subject relationship.

What statements would you add?

____

____

____

Exceptionality

Exceptionality has to do with happiness. People are trying to find happiness by striving for that unusual difference. This is out of control.

Athletes are told that only exceptional performance is acceptable. The boss expects 110% output on the job. Many spend money beyond their ability to repay.

The person who engages in exceptional behavior does not expect it to have an impact on themselves. Placing themselves in the exceptional category, they think that they ought to be immune from the outcome. An example of this is the person who smokes, and believes their health will not be affected.

Those who believe themselves to be exceptional live accordingly, and generally believe they are exempt from the consequences of their choices. In their belief, to be average is to live a boring and colorless life. They exist to live above this level they see as mediocre.

The problem is that the only time these people are happy is when they are being exceptional. Exceptional means infrequent. Therefore, happiness and fulfillment will be transitory, and ultimately frustrating.

Average Person

Who are the "average" people? They are the ones who make things work. They do not strive to be outstanding. I see them happily mowing their lawns, involved with their children, puttering around their yards, whistling. I see them in the kitchen. They are the postal worker, the grocery clerk, the gas attendant. I say, they, as average people, are happy most of the time.

Contrasted with exceptional people, I prefer to nest with the average. I believe I will be the happier for it.

Right or wrong judgments and inflammatory language

Right or wrong judgments: We hear the expression; "He is wrong." The dictionary defines wrong as: not in accordance with moral law, wicked, or whatever is not right or just. What we have said is, "I disagree with him." We have made a moral judgment. We ought not make moral judgments so easily. Maybe on clear matters (such as murder), but to elevate ordinary behavior to that same level is destroying our ability to make a distinction.

If someone disagrees with us they have disagreed with our morals. Our moral codes are set in childhood. Who is this who would question our moral values? Indignation is the reaction. The result is that the communication process stops. We will not listen to someone who determines that our moral values are "Wrong".

Inflammatory words: those that cause a reaction in our physical body. Adrenaline flows, the jaw tightens, the stomach turns, knots form, our hands clench into fists. Our society is so rife with this language that we've become numb to it. I would suggest we find other words that will do the same job, but not cause this physical reaction.

Words that come to mind that are inflammatory and judgmental are: right: wrong, weird, fair, queer, guilty, honest, fault, and blame. The people who use these words make a moral determination of what your values represent.

The better and neutral usage would be:

For right and wrong (judged or judging), substitute correct and incorrect.
For guilt (the state of having done wrong), substitute "I have broken one of my codes."
For honest (fair-dealing), substitute "take at face value."
For fault and blame (guilty of, error, failing), substitute the question, "What happened?"

Power bases — apart from the current relationship

A power base is an outside influence that makes a difference in the relationship. Where both parties are not a part of the decision-making process that influences the relationship, one of the parties is forced into a helpless position.

Several years ago, I knew a woman who was not getting the kind of cooperation she wanted from her husband regarding the care of their child. She discussed her feelings with a friend and decided not to have any more children. She then chose to have her tubes tied. There was no discussion with her husband on a decision that affected both their lives. The husband loved children and wanted more. She had the operation. He was in a helpless position.

It is not healthy to have a power base outside the relationship. When one discusses areas of difficulty with an outside party, they are working things out with the outside influence. There is little chance that changes will occur. If the troubles of the relationship are worked out within the relationship, only then can change happen. This section is for those who have strong desires to discuss their troubles with outsiders. I would say that you are being a coward. The discussion must be with the partner to create change.

Sometimes we all have a compelling desire for a "sounding-board." We have no expectation of resolution, nor do we really seek advice. Often, we simply want to verbalize our thoughts, to hear with our own ears the "brain static" and make some "sense" of it. If a "sounding board" is all you seek, it is incumbent upon you to inform the listener of this intention.

Making a difference

I believe that making a difference in others lives contributes to a positive self-image. I contend that our actions toward others, in part, affect our sense of value and determine whether we are satisfied with who we are. Suppose you want something of considerable value. You would not expect a friend, or family member, to provide it. Then someone does come forward with a gift of this item. It is freely given. Are you able to freely receive? Most of us have been taught that there is no free lunch. This may be generally true, but when a sincere person offers a gift, they have already been remunerated, by their own act of giving. They have made a difference in someone else's life, and by so doing, have enriched their own. This action gives them an increased sense of value, and validates their worth.

"Who have you chosen to be?"

We all have choices. Whatever our upbringing, whatever we think society has done, we can choose how we will produce ourselves. It is the conscious choices that make us what we are. Whatever you ***DO*** is your first choice. We all have ideas, but those ideas only have power as we act on them. ***YOU*** have the power to practice what *you* will become.

List the choices that define who you are.

____

____

____

____

____

____

My additions to this chapter

____

____

____

____

____

____

____

Chapter 2

Observations and Statements

How Things Are

In my experience, we are initially attracted to another person by looks. Something entices us: The eyes, the smile, an expression, the clothes, or some other physical characteristic. It seems that the next step is what is commonly called the "spark" of attraction. I wish to propose a theory of what that spark is. The sense of danger within us is often connected to a sensation in our chest; our heart starts pounding or our stomach tightens. Often there is a big emotional upheaval we call attraction, but it is actually a reaction to fear. The butterflies are a danger signal. The fear arises because we are putting ourselves in a vulnerable position. May I suggest that you examine that "spark" to determine if you are being driven by fear or true affinity. To assume that this "spark" is allure may cause us to find ourselves waking one morning, years later, next to a stranger we don't even ***like***, much less love. Next stop… a parting of the ways.

A Sorry State of Affairs

A generation ago, the following discussion would not have taken place. The topics we will discuss here are "new" problems. There were always isolated instances, but in the last two decades, these problems have become endemic. We have adopted a "new" language and "new" models to include behaviors and attitudes once thought to be bizarre. We are talking here about an aversion to being accountable, responsible, and willing to accept the consequences of our choices. Irresponsible; even violent or criminal behaviors, are written-off as the result of some past victimization. This is not meant in any way to trivialize legitimate circumstances of victimization. But, it need not take center stage in one's life and become the driving force of all future decisions and relationships.

Too many use their "past" as an excuse for unacceptable behavior in the present. It seems that the bottom line is that we have become people who no longer believe we need be accountable to anyone but ourselves. We are shielded from the consequences of our choices by overindulgent (or absent) parents. The state or federal governments provide loopholes for fiscal irresponsibility; i.e. welfare, food stamps, free medical care, subsidized housing, retirement, and bankruptcy. Physical irresponsibility is advocated by free condom and needle distributions, as well as on-demand abortions. Young men who once felt some obligation to marry the mothers of their children, or at least financially support them, have become an endangered species. Something has gone horribly awry when people will put their lives on the line to save an ancient tree, or the whales, but have no regard for the sanctity of human life. When abortion and euthanasia no longer cause a moral dilemma, maybe our standard has shifted too far.

Stop here. Do you have a moral code? How was that code developed? Does this code require that you be accountable? To whom are you accountable? Does your code require you to take responsibility for your life choices? If you could not satisfactorily answer the above questions, ***stop again***. This is important. It colors all other aspects of your life, and you owe it to yourself and everyone you know to put your moral code in place. ***Right now!***

I believe in...

I can support this belief by these reasons...

How Things Ought To Be

By this point, you should have at least formulated a rough sketch of your moral code. With this in place, you are now in a position to define your priorities. Take some time now, to write a list of prioritized values. (This is ***not*** a "wish" list). Once you have compiled your list, candidly assess what you lack to make your "list" a reality in your everyday life. If you have been irresponsible, for instance, what steps might you take to correct this?

Describe the areas where you fall short of the ***"goal"*** on your list. Beside each shortcoming, discuss the actions you'll need to implement to attain your desired goal. When you've completed this exercise, I have another one for you.

Shortcomings	***Action***

In generations past, a handshake or a verbal agreement was a bond and seal. It would have been unthinkable for a person not to keep their word. Can you be taken at your word? If you make a contract, can you be trusted to follow through?

This next exercise is a contract. I want you to write a contract with yourself. Define all the goals you set forth above, include them in your contract as commitments to yourself. Amazingly, when you instill integrity within yourself, you will find it an easy thing to keep integrity with others. It can become a habit and is a most worthwhile one to develop.

How comfortable would you be having a friend assess your moral character? Would you be comfortable having this friend point out your weaknesses? Do you trust this friend's judgments? If you are having difficulty developing your code, whom could you enlist to aid you?

____

____

____

____

____

Love is

I contend that the definition of love is "a looking back in appreciation of the other." We must have a history upon which to base our sense. You must first notice, then appreciate what the other has done to be able to love them. To appreciate another we must have had a positive record. Far too early, most of us define those feelings of giddiness, lust, infatuation, or excitement, as love.

There appear to be two sides of this love process: "in control" and "out of control."

> ***In control:*** when a person notices another and voluntarily focuses their attention. They develop an interest that can lead to an appreciation. If the experiences have meaning, bring joy, and are positive; love develops naturally.
>
> ***Out of control:*** is characterized by statements such as:
> "I was struck by" (an involuntary act)
> "I was drawn to" (an involuntary act)
> "Like a magnet"
> "I need you"
> "I fell hopelessly in love with"
> "Out of nowhere"

There is no natural progression, no time for a deep rooting, and little substance or strength.

The out-of-control person pushes for quick involvement. There is a hastening for an exclusive commitment almost immediately. These relationships wither in a crisis.

Do you fall in love easily?
Yes?/Why ______________________________

No?/Why ______________________________

Feelings — *versus* — Ideas

"I feel that I ought to..." When we try to discuss with someone their statements that use the expression "I feel," we are unable to disagree. The reason is that by disagreeing we say, "Your feelings are not valid." Who are we to determine the validity of someone else's feelings? If the subject is proposed as an idea, we then have a basis for persuasive discussion. Ideas can be discussed. The usage of "I feel" instead of "my idea" creates a communication vacuum. "Feelings" are generated as "an individual physical determination," and as such, are not always grounded in fact, and often lack logic and reason. An "idea," on the other hand, contains aggregate information and facts, and may include some level of emotion or feeling, but is not grounded upon the shifting sands of sensation. Your communication efforts will be more successful if you will sort out for yourself the difference between your feelings (physical determinations) and your ideas (opinions).

This is not meant to assert that feelings should never be shared. It is meant, rather, to serve as a caution. Determine, first, whether you are open to discuss "ideas" or share "feelings."

If you are looking for a term that conveys more than an idea, or an emotion, use "sense." The senses include our perceptions of the physical, emotional, spiritual, religious, opinions, and judgments.

Needs — *versus* — Wants

We hear the term "I need...(this or that)" This is one of many misused statements common today. Let's look at what distinguishes a need from a want.

> ***Need***: These are the physical requirements that sustain life. They include: air, water, food, and protection from the elements and from predators. It is further supposed that nurturing of infants is necessary for normal development.
>
> Other areas of need might be: mental or spiritual nourishment.
>
> Though we can survive with only the physical needs fulfilled, life would be grim without some desires being met.
>
> ***Want***: every other desire.
>
> The confusing of needs and wants creates poor communication. The degree of importance is misconstrued. We are placing a value on ordinary wants and elevating them to a basic need.
>
> When you tell another "I need..." you put them in a position to deny you a basic requirement of life. What you are

usually talking about is a desire for something. You are shifting the responsibility for fulfilling your desires to a higher level than it warrants. You are not entitled to a "want."

Is there entitlement for a need? Why?

____

____

____

____

____

____

I know my rights

There appear to be two types of rights:

Basic: Everyone is entitled to the right of safety, protection, love, freedom *(that does not impinge on another)*, and the basic needs.

Earned: A level of augmented rights that would be earned. They would include procreation, intrusive-freedom *(ability to intervene)*, and the privilege to govern.

I am going to make the assumption that rights *(beyond the basics)* are gained as a direct result of responsibility. To further enhance the thought; the larger the responsibility, the more rights an individual ought to have.

Have you heard the phrase "noblesse oblige?" Simply stated, it means that nobility obligates. In this is the assumption that the higher the authority, the more significant the responsibility. It then follows that more rights are accorded as well.

Children given additional rights or privileges at each stage of maturing develop into adults better equipped to exercise those within reasonable bounds. When raising our children, we increased responsibility and rights proportionate to one another. Just becoming a year older in no way accorded privileges unless there was enough maturity to also assume the responsibilities attached.

Has our government, in an attempt at "fairness," gone overboard in this arena of "rights?" We hear about the rights of criminals versus victims; the right of the unborn versus the woman's; homosexuals versus heterosexuals; church versus state; free speech versus pornography; (and the list goes on). It seems that in an attempt to be all things to all people, someone will have their rights abridged. How far is too far?

The other day I ran into a friend who was relating that at work they were subject to a "federal compliance audit." She is employed at a mental institution. All the patients were to be informed and made to understand that they had the following three rights: to marry, to procreate, and to divorce. My question was, "If a thirty year old was deemed to have the mental capacity of a seven year old, would these rights be available to them? If so, then, who takes care of the children, does the shopping, or drives the car? Who does all of those other tasks of daily living that are being taken care of for them in the institution?"

The obvious answer is what is left unsaid. Though they may have the *right* to procreate, most states have mechanisms in place through their social service agencies that preclude these parents from having custody because of the very problems stated above. Is this a deceptive practice to hold out the hope and joy of parenthood without informing them that, though they may bear children, in most cases they will not be allowed to keep them?

Who writes these government directives? The answer: ***Not*** your elected officials. Therefore, as a populace, we are afforded little or no say in matters that could impact us directly.

Civilized societies have created laws to put a cap on how far one may "exercise" their rights, which is appropriate. But, be forewarned: governmental agencies *(individuals within the agencies)* enact policies daily which carry the force of law without the consent of the electorate.

Have you had an experience where someone exercising their "rights" abridged yours?

Cursing up a storm

Last night I heard a person use some very offensive language. The words were directed at another. They were very angry. I thought: "Do they realize how foolish they appear?" I empathize with the one suffering this insult. They were too polite, or, could it be, too mature, to cuss back.

It should be stated that the one being verbally accosted had two choices: respond *or* ignore the insults. Responses could be further broken down to include: in-kind, subtle, sarcastic, or reasonable. Any form of cursing, insults, or hateful language, is verbal battery. As children, we learn that our language promotes a response or reaction in others. It is said for effect to parents, siblings, and peers. At some stage, however, a mature person realizes that words can be and often are damaging, not only to the one to whom they are directed, but to the speaker. Words once spoken cannot be taken back. The adage "You can't un-ring a bell" comes to mind.

A wiser man than I once stated that it isn't what a man puts in his mouth that defiles him, but rather, what comes out of his mouth. I can't think of a better way to put it than that.

What are your thoughts?

Smoking?

What are your views? If you smoke you have to know that to a nonsmoker you stink. Your clothes smell, and you know that you have bad breath. Your car and home have a bar-room odor and your pet confuses you with a fireplace. To most, your addiction creates a sense of pity for you. They do not want you to die horribly, unable to breath.

Does nagging a smoker stop the habit? Can you think of something that would be effective?

Date or Ego Boost

I would like to discuss the concept of "Ego Dating." We all want to impress another. When we are interested in someone we want them to think that we are a good choice for them. We go to great lengths to impress that person, but when it comes to daily living, we are unable to keep up the effort. I would caution that we try not to make too much of an early impression, but to be as we are every other day. If you have to put out extraordinary effort for the early dating period, how will you keep it up, and how can you top it? I believe that this is what will cause those statements, "You used to bring me flowers," "We used to go out more," or "You used to like sex." The window-dressing creates the expectation of its continuation.

Could this be a subtle form of deception?

"Yes, No... Maybe"

Men seem to be more direct in stating intentions. Women more often consider other's feelings over their own. When a man shows interest in a woman, and it is not mutual, she tries to spare his feelings. She says something like, "I'm busy, right now". What ought to be said is "No, thanks, I'm not interested." Any sentence that does not contain the word "*No*," is heard as *Maybe*. We all know that *Maybe* contains the possibility that it could change to a *Yes*. Many of us keep pursuing in hopes of consent. I would much rather hear a direct yes or no. Do ***not*** send mixed signals: say what you mean, and mean what you say. Then *yes* and *no* messages will not be misunderstood.

Women generally have a tougher time being clear about their wants, desires, or feelings. Most were taught to acquiesce to others or be seen as selfish.

What "maybe" statements have you made rather than give a clear yes or no?

Stay with a Jerk?

There are several reasons why someone would stay with a jerk. Some of these are: emotional overload, habit, training (upbringing), poor examples by peers, father or mother offered no emotional support, thinking we can't attract another, just don't know better, or fear that crises will ensue, (financial strain, being alone, taking sole responsibility for tasks that the other had attended to, possible retaliation, etc.). And, here's one you might not have expected, laziness!!

Have you stayed in a relationship longer than you should have? Fully discuss why.

Setups and Hook

An acquaintance said: "I need to use your car to go to Portland (150 miles away) to pick up my Christmas present."

Wayne: "But it's only April. What is going on?"

Acquaintance: "I have to go Monday night to get it. I need your car."

Wayne: "Why?"

Acquaintance: "This is the only time I can get my gift. It's very important to me."

Wayne: "Please explain why you 'need' my car."

I am going to stop here in this conversation and talk about what seems to be going on. To use the word *"need"* has elevated whatever this is to the same level as air and water or a life sustaining substance. For me to say "no" denies them these life substances.

For the acquaintance to use Christmas puts me on the spot. It is as if they are asking, "Do you believe in Christmas?" It would be implied that if I don't, that I am a grinch. "Would you deny me 'my' Christmas present?"

Now comes the tie in, the hook.

Acquaintance: "My son got tickets to the basketball game. He paid over $100. for them. Just he and I are going. It is my Christmas present. You wouldn't keep me from going, would you?"

If I say no, the hook is?

Individuals often resort to ploys to get their way in relationships. These have obviously been successful in the past, or they wouldn't continue to be used. One scenario might go like this:

> ***She:*** I am so glad you love and trust me.
> ***He:*** Huh!
> ***She***: All of my girlfriends are getting together this weekend at the coast. Julie can't go. Her husband won't let her.
> ***He:*** Yes honey, I trust you.
> ***She:*** Gail rented this cabin at a bargain price, so we will only have to pay $20 each.
> ***He:*** That certainly is cheap.
> ***She:*** You told me that you wanted to wax your boat this weekend and it'll be just us girls. *(hesitation)* You don't mind if I go, do you?
> ***He:*** Well…
> ***She:*** I made this casserole just for you. All you have to do is pop it in the microwave. *(quickly)* Do you want to mess around tonight?
> ***He:*** …

So where are the setups and the hooks? Define what other major issues are going on.

____

____

____

____

____

____

____

____

____

____

____

____

____

Lest we direct this dubious manipulating solely at women, let us pose another illustration which will sound all too familiar to most women, and perhaps a few men.

> Teenage couple on a date. He says, "Let me drive you up to the top of that hill to see the city lights. The view is really great. We can listen to some nice music and talk awhile." *(Fast forward 30-45 minutes).*
> He is beginning to get excited, starts groping, and is sure that if his desires are not met immediately, he will surely die. He says, "What's wrong? Don't you trust me? I would never do anything to hurt you. No one will ever know, and I will still respect you." She continues to resist. He says, "But, if you *Really* loved me, you'd want to make me happy."

What form of manipulation is he using to get his way?

About Control

A favorite saying of mine is: "I only run me." By making this statement often, it acts as a reminder. It keeps me on track, lest I forget and try to run another. With past relationships rife with control issues, we missed out on so much. We are always trying to run the other.

Now I am very comfortable giving advice, when asked, and not having expectations that it be followed. I only run me; they run themselves, so whatever action they take is theirs.

If I am trying to control another, who is in charge of me? No one; so then I must be out of control.

Name ways others try to control us.

Name areas where you find difficulty relinquishing control. Suggestions include; parenting, money, decorating, running the home, and relationships.

Harmony

A common cry today among the recently divorced is, "When I started dating this time everything seemed to have changed. When I dated before, it appeared that almost everyone I knew had a common background. Today, those I meet are so diverse in thought and philosophy." We have had a lot of change. The differences can range from conflicting views on the Civil Rights Movements, Safe Sex, Who Calls Who, to the Citizens Alliance. Some of the alternate life-styles range are from the bizarre to the unreal. Those I spend time with must have life-styles similar to mine. I find that when I "fit in" I am most comfortable. Harmony is what is important to me. New ideas and variety may be the spices that keep couples interested, but I find the glue of the relationship is what couples have in common. A certain amount of diversity is acceptable, but we should seek relationships that produce harmony, not discord. Your cumulative life experience colors your world view. Is your partner coloring from the same Crayola® box?

Do I want glue or spice? Can I have both?

We Communicate

Face it; we do a poor job of communicating, and we all set up expectations that are not met. We haven't learned how to ask for what would fulfill us, and we're mostly frustrated for all our efforts. We ask for sensitivity, vulnerability, and truthfulness, but are we prepared to accept what we've requested, without standing in judgment of the content?

What environment have you fostered to promote the safe sharing of sensitive issues? What changes would you make to facilitate candid communication?

____

____

____

____

____

____

____

____

Packrats and World Travelers

We all know what a packrat is: one who keeps everything and throws nothing away. A world traveler, on the other hand, knows all too well that he must pack light, leaving behind all but the essentials. Is all of your baggage essential? What old hurts, resentments, and pain have you religiously packed, unpacked, sorted, examined, and worn as a badge of courage? Often included in our baggage are old tools that used to work for us. When will we see these for what they are… out-dated, polyester stuff we long ago outgrew?

Our carry-on baggage often determines how we communicate, whether we are able to operate with integrity or not, and a myriad of other factors. Have you fallen into the in-vogue trap of "victim" mentality, abandonment, abuse, etc. It is not intended here to minimize being abused, abandoned, or victimized. What I am addressing is the *"wearing"* of these experiences as excuses for dysfunctional behavior. No one has responsibility for your life but *you*. Have you rationally responded to your life challenges, or have you reacted? Take a few moments to think this through. There is a distinct difference between response and reaction. Define these terms from your frame of reference.

A response is:

A reaction is:

I am Alone

At the beginning of a solitary walk (particularly for those who have been recently divorced or separated), there is little distinction between being alone and being lonely. We are too close to the crisis that precipitated this solitary-ness. The word "alone" has no positive connotation. We hear "alone," and we conjure a picture of lonely. After time, we progress through the various stages of this new existence, and hopefully attain a new perspective. "Alone" becomes a sanctuary, not a solitary confinement. There was once an attitude that we each were halves of a perfect whole, and that we only needed to find our "soul mate" to find fulfillment. We are finally discovering that two perfectly whole individuals make for a more healthy relationship.

Do I engage in "I am lonely" language?

Yes ❑ ***No*** ❑ ***Only when it gets me mileage*** ❑

Loose Lips

During World War II this statement was bandied about: "Loose lips sink ships." That could be said of relationships, too. When did it become acceptable to share information told in confidence? When did we get the idea that intimate details of our relationships were fodder for the public trough?

There are two scenarios that come to mind where this tactic is employed: by "telling tales out of school", the teller believes themselves elevated above the "told on"; in scene two, there is a seeking of approval, or an ally. Though you may wish to make elements of your life "fishbowl" entertainment, do you suppose you have the "right" to hold your partner up to that scrutiny without permission? Would you presume to be comfortable knowing that your partner is sharing information about you without your permission?

Take a moment to think about how you've operated in past relationships. Have you kept intimate details to yourself, or are you a "ship sinker?"

____

____

____

____

____

Relationship Roulette

Try something. Cover my – a, b, c answers and give your response to the following relationship "what-we-tell-others-about-what-we-are-doing" questions.

One view
No, I'm not looking
a.) Right now
b.) Ever
c.) Not for you, anyway
One view
I'm not looking, but.
a.) If a millionaire asks
b.) If you act serious, I'll reconsider
c.) If I'm single toooo long, well…
One view
I'm looking for a serious relationship.
a) I don't like being alone.
b) I'm not really, but this scares most off
c) and you'll do just fine

What did you tell your last date? What did he or she tell you? You were there, weren't you?

____
____
____
____
____
____

Spiritual, Religious, Atheist or Agnostic

Our religious views are based on deep conviction. ***Whoa***... to those who ignore the beliefs of another. Worse yet... is to say, "Your beliefs are not valid."

For a solid foundation, the Golden Rule ought be the basis of most relationships. Whether the belief system is more formal, and organized, or loosely held and practiced, it must be acknowledged as valid. You need not be religious to appreciate that if the Golden Rule were universally practiced, it would go a long way to end conflict.

Briefly describe your religious outlook. Do you think that there is a difference between religious and spiritual?

____
____
____
____
____
____
____
____
____
____

Land Mines

BOOM! Just moving along what appears to be a smooth road, not looking for shocks, or explosions. ***Surprise!*** Land mines are everywhere, and you are not aware of them until the damage is done. Bouncing Betty will blow your foot off before you know it. ***WARNING!*** Watch your step. Tread lightly here. What may lurk just below the surface? Prudence dictates that you walk circumspectly until you're very familiar with the terrain.

The above refers to those with a blase attitude, or a naivete which assumes that unless there are evidences of problems, none exist. Relationships require thoughtful attendance and a commitment to awareness. One who is watchful will not miss or ignore the warning signs of danger, or the potential subsurface detonators.

Let's look at this from another perspective. Everyone goes through those days and periods when they are angry, sad, unhappy, etc..., for no apparent reason; yet these transitory dips are not necessarily fatal to a relationship. When, however, these transient times are not tended appropriately, there is a high potential of a pattern developing like a cancer. In the early stages, the patient seems to be asymptomatic, yet they have the cancer nonetheless. Only when the painful symptoms appear, and the diagnosis of terminal illness is given, is real attention paid to the condition.

Simply stated, the foregoing says: pay attention; be quick to listen and slow to judge.

Permission

By definition: authorization, allowance, consent, or approval. We are talking about giving choices. If, for instance, you wish to broach a painful subject, a preface might be: "Would you be comfortable discussing...?" There are difficulties in all of our lives that may have caused trauma. When we know that it may be difficult for another to address a subject, ask first. They may not want to broach that matter, and you could cause harm you never intended. To request permission causes no harm and may avoid unnecessary discomfort.

This in no way negates the responsibility to intervene when the behaviors of the other pose a threat to their lives, or those of minor children; i.e. drinking and driving, drug addiction, or other reckless actions.

Keep in mind, not ***All*** things have to be discussed.

Would you seek permission at any time?

Kissing

This is usually a physical expression of caring (though in some cultures it is used merely as a form of greeting). The level of intensity may vary depending on the situation. For each circumstance, we develop a style. Let's look at the differing styles.

Family: The family style is taught by our parents. Have you thought about why they did it this way? Would there be another technique that you can use?

Acquaintance: The range is from gushy kissing to a peck on the cheek. How do you handle acquaintances?

Friendship: Are displays of affection or greeting acceptable among your friends?

Lover: as long as the event matches or exceeds the expectation, we're okay. But what about the remedial kisser? What do you do? You can't really suggest lessons, can you?

There are as many kinds of kisses as there are levels of passion. Non passionate: a gentle lingering whisper is very pleasant. The progression to another phase must take a period of time. To leap into passion quickly is what happens too often. Non-passionate does not include French kissing. Point of fact: French kissing every time leaves nothing for the more passionate encounter. If this is your M.O., you may be implying that you are only interested in passion.

Passionate: do you want to seek permission first? Permission can be implied or verbal. A style usually develops between two lovers. Has your style just happened, or was there conversation about what is pleasing?

____

____

____

____

____

____

____

I Love You

If he/she says "I love you" what is your response? For me, some of the thoughts that race through my conscious mind are: Does she define love the same way I do? Have we really known one another long enough for this to happen? Is it just the passion of the moment? Help! I'm scared. What now?

Love is a process that cannot be rushed. Feelings of the heart may take months or years to mature. Each person must define when they sense love.

Many factors affect how you'll respond to this scenario. Let's look at some of these, then take a few moments to see what other factors you might add to the list. ***When***: Was it so soon, you were barely "off the lot?" Or, has it been so long you're ready to join the 100,000 mile club? If so, consider an "option to buy" at this point, a stroke of good fortune, because your warranty expired some time ago. ***Where***: In a public place or somewhere private where discussion of such matters is appropriate? Is the locale "romantic" and of such influence that at another location this subject would not have come up? Are you both sober and in control of your faculties? The world ***does*** look different through the bottom of a highball glass! ***How***: Was this a spontaneous utterance or has it been well-considered? Often, professions in a moment of spontaneous passion sound different over coffee the next morning.

The advice is: Share what is in your heart. There is a risk, but if you do not declare your beliefs, the other may be too frightened to profess theirs, and you may never know what might have been.

For your consideration: You've been seeing someone for about three months. The relationship is relaxed, you have a good time together, and enjoy many common activities. You even share a common world view. At dinner one evening, your date professes undying love for you. How will you respond? What thought processes will you go through? If you've never considered this type of scenario, do so now. Chances are good that one similar could occur in your dating lifetime.

How will I respond?

I love you.

Do you love me?

How much do you love me?

The Vine That Clings

We have all had the experience of being held beyond a comfort level, by family, friends, acquaintances, or lovers. Should we be more sensitive to one another's body language? Or should we be asking permission at each encounter? Is this a fit topic for discussion early in a relationship? Are there boundaries that are fixed, or are some flowing? This topic gave rise to a good bit of discussion around the office when it was broached. I sensed some differing ideas along gender lines. What's your thinking on this subject?

Some times we all require a little extra assurance that we are loved and appreciated, but a consistent pattern may signal some image problems that should be addressed. What constitutes a clinger? You define what levels generally fall within your comfort zone.

How much assurance (reassurance) is average?

The "Two — Man — Woman" and The "Two — Woman — Man"

The man or woman engaging in this game is operating with an inflated ego. They have attached too much importance to engaging in what they perceive as fun. This stress causes all sides of the triangle to be weakened. There is no way to partner with another if there are three involved. Someone is always "odd man out" and probably all are missing out on something. The excuse often is: "I love them both"; "I am so confused"; or "I cannot make up my mind". Of course not! A decision was made to suspend rational thinking. At some point you had a choice of whether or not to engage in this selfishness. When you continue self-indulgence long enough, you sear off the wise counsel of your own intuition.

What would you say to someone if they used this ploy?

Will You Marry Me?

The big question. Any woman will recall what she was wearing, where she was, what her thoughts were, and what he did, at the time she was asked.

This moment can become a memorable milestone, or a recurring nightmare. How do we make it a positive memory? Do we ask our friends what to do and say? Do we dive right in, improvising as we go? We guys know if we don't do it "right" we're in trouble!

How long has the couple known each other? When is it prudent to start considering a marriage? One day is too soon certainly, but would you know someone well enough in three months, six or twelve?

Here are some statements that I have heard were used:

"Marry me."

"Please marry me."

"I'm pregnant. Are you going to marry me?"

"I'm pregnant. You do not have to marry me."

"I love you. Marry me."

"If you don't marry me, I'm going to move out."

"Do you think that we should get married?"

(to the parents) "Can I marry your daughter?"

"So, you want to get married?"

"I have carefully considered that I am in love with you. I have known you for six months and find that I have grown to love you deeply. I would like to spend the remaining years of my life with you. With these thoughts in mind… will you marry me?"

How would you ask?

Does the person being asked just say yes? Maybe they could elaborate on what their feelings and thoughts are? What of the person that was drunk and asked? What if a romantic setting had been prepared?

How would you respond?

Does the man always have to ask the woman? Why?

The man or woman may say no. What a dilemma, I do not know of a non-awkward retort to "no."

Write your retort to "no".

If you have purchased an engagement ring you may loose a lot of money. I might suggest that one might ask for the marriage and then pick out the engagement ring... together.

How do you set a limit on the amount to spend for rings?

My additions to this chapter

Chapter 3

What's in it for me?

The motivations to form relationships

The reasons we form relationships often change as we age. There are motivators that seem to be part of the fabric of our human species. These are not necessarily "will-driven." There also appear to be some very "stage-specific" motivators that result from conscious decisions of will.

These stages are: 1) infant, 2) toddler, 3) adolescent, 4) young adult, 5) adult, 6) mid-life, 7) senior, 8) aged, 9) infirm.

There are not always clear borders. Some motivators operate in more than one stage, whether they originate naturally, or are chosen.

This exercise is meant to awaken in you a desire to research your intentions and determine whether you are operating with the appropriate motivators for your stage. We often see, for example, adolescents having babies in an attempt to live beyond their years and experience, or those in mid-life acting out adolescent behaviors in an attempt to "recapture" their youth. Either way, I hope this exercise will serve as a catalyst for thought.

Fundamental Reasons for a Relationship Diagram	
Stage	General Motivator
Infant	survival, pleasure
Toddler	survival, ego development
Adolescent	sexual awakening
Young Adult	independence, procreation
Adult	*(you fill in motivators)*
Mid-life	*(you fill in motivators)*
Senior	*(you fill in motivators)*
Aged	*(you fill in motivators)*
Infirm	survival

Stage Reasons for Relationships Diagram

Stage	Specific Motivator
Infant	socialization, comfort
Toddler	socialization, comfort
Adolescent	approval, ego, social, gain
Young Adult	fulfillment, gain, companionship
Adult	financial, social, sexual, ego
Mid-life	fear of being alone, financial, social
Senior	caregiver, companion, financial
Aged	caregiver, companion, financial
Infirm	caregiver, companion

You can fill in several more Specific Motivators in the above chart.

Obviously, we have not listed all possible motivations. What others might you add? Are your motivations stage-appropriate? If you find your motivations are more appropriate to an adolescent, are you willing to work on emotional growth?

My additions to this chapter

Chapter 4

Who Am I? What Do I Want?

Before we begin, a few words should be said about how we define who we are.

There is a temptation to list the different roles we assume in our lives as who we are. In this section, however, we are looking for attributes of character, not roles. For instance, if you are a corporate executive, a father, a bowler, or a dog trainer; these are differing roles you assume, but they do not constitute who you are. Are you gregarious, sensitive, compassionate, spiritual, contemplative, etc.? The "Who you are" list should detail your character traits. Be candid. Don't just list your positive attributes. If you are hot-tempered, jealous, and contentious, list these as well. Maybe they aren't wonderful traits, but if you acknowledge them, you can always change them.

1) Relational Skills

Conflict

Are you a conflict avoider? Have you shunned conflict resolution, or did you think those two words were mutually exclusive? Are you afraid to broach subjects that present a potential for disagreement? Is this avoidance behavior a trait to be nurtured, or would you and your partner benefit from some changes in this area? A conflict is a conflict, whether it is spoken or not. An unspoken conflict simply hides beneath the surface, feeding on itself; growing ever larger. You can bet that it will sprout at some time in the future, and will be considerably larger than in the beginning. Take that thing out and expose it to the light of day; discuss it. There is a risk associated with this, but it will prove to be worth it every time. Take the initiative. The conflict will not resolve itself. Doing the "ostrich" thing is not healthy. Keep your head in the sand too long and you're guaranteed to suffocate.

In this space list your positive and negative character attributes, and your relational skills, or lack of them. This will create a springboard for further action.

What habits pose a conflict?

With a well established habit, we do not have to think, we just do it. Initially there may have been some thought put into the action, but over time, we have entered into a non-thinking situation. What may not be offensive to ourselves may impact another beyond that which we believe to be reasonable. Over the course of time, habits (some innocent) may become mountains in another's eyes. Does he or she have irritating habits such as:

Squeezing the toothpaste from the center?
Unrolling the toilet paper over the top, or under the roll?
Not lowering the toilet seat after use?
Leaves dishes in the kitchen sink?
Does not call when they are going to be late?
Belches, let's gas escape to gain attention?
Throws their dirty laundry on the floor?
Slaps me on the behind in public?
They blow their nose with their hand?
Interrupts my conversation in public?
Teases the cat?
Tickles my feet?
Told an 'out of place' story at the office party?
Pops their knuckles?
Is always late?
Does not fill the gas tank when it is empty?
They always are giving advice?
Will not put the lid on the shampoo?
You fill in the last items.

____
____
____
____
____
____

Women Complain

Real Men: can sit down. The number one complaint I hear from female friends is, "The most disgusting job I have to do is to clean up the urine dribbles off of the commode." "Why must men stand to urinate?" Since mothers usually do the potty training, maybe they should take the initiative and teach their sons to sit.

For you who question the statement about women teaching their children: yes, men can assume this responsibility, but if you want the job done, don't depend on another *to do it.*

Real Men stand and women sit. This is clearly a matter of control and power, i.e.; the dominant person stands.

The questions were posed: Is it an instinctive thing to stand? Might there be a tremendous amount of peer pressure to stand? How about men cleaning the commode? Does standing make men macho? And, who decided to put carpeting in the bathroom?

Men Complain

> "Now that I'm hooked, we don't spend time together doing what I enjoy." Most men like engaging in activities with their female companions. In many relationships, after a period of time, the recreational companionship wanes. For some, it is separate vacations; for others, there is no leisure time together. Some relationships will not suffer with an arrangement like this, while for others it is evidence of avoidance.

Women: what activities do you share with your male partner?

Petty Issues

In the scope of things, some stuff is really small. The problem is, that added together, all these straws… you get the picture. Who will take responsibility for keeping the garden weeded? What petty issues have you given power to?

"The laundry sits in the basket, not folded. Can't he see that it needs to be put away?"

"He should know that his behavior bothers me. We've been together a long time. He should know what I think."

"I shouldn't have to tell her I love her. She knows."

Do you believe that your partner should be able to read your mind? What do you assume that he or she should just "know?"

Have I been the one to enable?

An enabler (in this sense) is one who facilitates the continuation of destructive behaviors. By enabling, you sanction and give power to those behaviors. If you have been partnered with someone in the past who engaged in destructive behaviors, take a moment to assess whether you condoned or ignored their actions.

Have I used the words "I am just trying to help…" when my intent is to control the situation?

Cherish?

Cherish: as described in Webster's, is "to protect and treat with affection: to entertain in the mind, hold in the heart, to nurse"

Do you cherish anyone? What actions do you take to make the act of cherishing overt?

2) Physical Characteristics

Beautiful

Being born physically beautiful is a real handicap. It creates a standard by which one's entire life is measured. Beautiful people have a difficult time separating their looks from their true worth. They especially have it tough when the ravages of time and gravity begin to change their once outstanding visage into something less than glamorous. Life is tougher for these people because they are born exceptional. They have usually never known what it is to be average.

Why are so many people looking for a beautiful partner? I maintain that it is a searching for, and a desire to be linked to the exceptional.

Physically attractive

This category is peopled by those who don't fall into the "drop dead" looks group, but they are pleasing to look at, and don't possess physical characteristics that seem out of place.

Just So

Not quite homely, yet physical attributes are not these folks' strong suit. You'll probably be attracted to these people by their personality or intellect. These folks have to work harder at being attractive because they don't possess many outstanding physical characteristics.

Not so Good

What can we say? Nearly homely. Not quite ugly? Extra effort needs to be made for this group to be "fetching." Grooming, clothing, personality, sense of humor, and an active mind are usually the best "makeup." So, if your life sucks, get out and do something about changing it.

Ugly

You may be beautiful inside; so, turn yourself inside out and let the world see what you're made of. It may take some effort on your part. You may have always been introverted and may want a public speaking class or some other tools to bring forth your shine.

This is what I am going to do to enhance the sense of my current physical appearance. I will write a detailed plan here and now.

Height

You are 4'10" and want to date a 6' beauty? Surveys show that short men are at a disadvantage in the mating scene. Many women want to be with a taller man; one that gives a sense of protection. Height equates to the ability to protect. This is one area where men have difficulty making a change to improve their situation. Short men do end up with some pretty wonderful women, but often they must work harder to find that mate.

Weight

She said, "I lost fifty pounds this past year." I said, "That's interesting. How did you do it?" She replied, "My doctor said that if I didn't lose fifty pounds, I would die! During my examinations he had found that I had diabetes; the additional weight was going to kill me. It was a matter of priorities." She addressed what was important, instant gratification or life. Are you serious enough about your life to reorder your priorities? Is instant gratification more important than your very life? Also, notice that this woman did not mention any magical diet she used to lose the weight.

> ***Six months later;*** You notice that she has added about twenty five pounds to her weight. In conversation she states, "I am so happy now that I'm with you that I just can't stop eating." What is going on here? Is it really true for her that happiness is the cause of her weight gain? Is it conversely true, then, that if she were not so happy, she would be thinner? Does this now make you responsible for her gain in weight? Isn't that a thought-provoking question? Think about it. If you're responsible, she's not. What a clever way to shift responsibility; by compliment.

For people with eating disorders, food has been vested with power beyond reason. Rationally, food is a neutral substance; with power only in the sense that it sustains our physical bodies. One's view of food, then, determines their relationship to it.

In the one extreme, the anorexic sees food as an enemy to be thwarted, while the overweight person sees food as a suitor to be wooed. Neither attitude is healthful. Often, there has been either a real or perceived event, and the emotional response to it determines who or what will be vested with power. The challenge, then, is to draw both extreme responses closer to the median.

The change to a more healthy position may be brought about by something as simple as stop!... there is no simple way to control weight. The best solution I have seen is to strictly adhere to a diabetic diet and to commit to an exercise program. What ever your choice, *it will be hard work.*

Mitigating Factors

What other things might be factored in to help balance out what you deem to be defects? How about: He's got Bill Gates' money, Mel Gibson's looks, a black belt in karate, a body by Jake, and a wardrobe by Guess? Sound shallow? Welcome to reality. You may not have the ability to go out tomorrow and amass a fortune, have extensive plastic surgery, or become Superman overnight, but what things on this list do you have control over?

Money

____

____

____

____

____

____

____

____

____

Surgery

Physical conditioning

Wardrobe

Esteem *Versus* — Image diagram	
Esteem *(what is)*	**Image** *(what appears to be)*
Intrinsic value or worth *(born with)*	Visible physical attributes *(appearance)*
Self-recognized: being alive and human gives me worth. ***Not recognized by self:*** *(available only – through other sources)*	***Self-concept:*** average height, slender, fair skinned, dark-haired, hazel eyes
Others recognize: my value as a human being. ***Others do not recognize:*** base my value on attributes rather than intrinsic worth	***Other's concept:*** taller than average skinny, attractive, pale, great smile

Esteem = Is our worth and value, as an entitlement at birth.

Image = What appears to be, to ourselves or to others.

Self-esteem ***does not*** equate to self-image. You should esteem yourself of worth and value because you are a part of the human race. Your self-image is who you see yourself to be.

What has traditionally been taught about self esteem is erroneous. This misinformation has caused many to devalue their worth. Untold heartache has been caused by "experts." Too many people have a diminished concept of their inherent value. We all have innate worth the moment we are conceived.

What your perceived character traits are differ with the degree of closeness you share with the perceiver. If we look at the life of a very public person, we often see what appears to be attractive attributes of character. This public persona, though, is rarely a true representation of what is. More often, it's media hype and promotion. Even the average individual, however, can project attributes that are an illusion.

To change how others perceive you most often requires changes first in you. Rarely will their perceptions of you change without new visual or verbal information.

If image is what ***appears to be***, not what ***is***, then image is mutable. If you have physical attributes that impact your life negatively, determine areas of possible change. Create a plan of change and implement the plan. Whether you're short or tall, you can create the illusion of height with the appropriate clothing, physical bearing, or hairstyle. If you are over- or underweight, clothing style and color can create the illusion of a more attractive appearance Physical appearance is one arena where significant changes are possible. Features can be mitigated by makeup or surgery for extreme cases. If you're motivated, speech patterns and communication styles can be improved.

Your self-concept is changeable. When you have a good grasp of essence, and a concrete understanding of your intrinsic worth, your concept of yourself will be more in line with what *is*.

Your sense of enhanced positive image will proportionally rise with your increased caring and accomplishments. We are not talking about "feel good", "politically correct" activities, but heartfelt efforts of persistence and commitment that build character.

Now do you see that what have been labeled as self-esteem issues are more image-related issues? So, let's see how you can work with it!

Make five columns. In the first, list factors that make up your image. The second column is for what you perceive the problem to be. In the third, list what is. In the fourth column, list any changes you'd make for each of the items in your first column. In the fifth column, list what you are willing to do to facilitate the transition. See the example on the next page.

My Image Change Form
(sample)

Image		What is	Possible	Changes
Factor	**Perception**			
Weight	I think that I am fat	230 lb.	Different clothing will mask my weight	Buy clothes to make me appear thinner
Wear glasses	I'm a nerd	Poor vision	Contact lenses	I'll see the eye doctor as soon as possible
Height	?	6' 5"?	?	?
Speech	?	?	?	?
Clothes	?	?	?	?
Teeth	?	Crooked?	?	?
Bald	?	?	?	?
Facial wart	?	?	Removal?	?
?	?	?	?	?

Your Image Change Form

Image		What is	Possible	Changes
Factor	Perception			

Clothes Make The . . . ?

In times past, great attention was paid to attire. One did not venture out without being appropriately dressed for the intended occasion. Today, with the ever-increasing popularity of blue jeans and other casual clothing, even many businesses allow for a 'dress down' day. Have you become blasé, paying little or no attention to your attire? Do you wear jeans for virtually all occasions? Are you comfortable in your cleanest dirty shirt? If you are dirty, sloppy, or still wearing plaid polyester bell-bottoms, you and your wardrobe will need an immediate update.

What changes will I make in my appearance?

What is my clothing budget?			
	pants	$__.__ each month at $__.__ each	
	shoes	$__.__ each month at $__.__ each	
	shirts	$__.__ each month at $__.__ each	
	?	$__.__ each month at $__.__ each	

Behavior

Whether behaviors or actions are overt or covert, they impact "community" at large. This "community" sets standards of what *is* and what *is not* acceptable. Actions adjudged as benefiting community are perceived as positive, while those determined as taking from community are perceived as negative. Both image and esteem appear to be influenced, though, in actuality, only the image should be affected. A person's true worth does not change moment-to-moment based on their action. Only our perception of their value may change.

To illustrate: a man and wife living in Iraq abide within a "community" which has a standard of acceptable behavior varying widely from Western countries. If the husband in Iraq slaps, or otherwise "disciplines," his wife, his community has adjudged this behavior as benefiting the community. In Western cultures this behavior is seen as battering and abusive. Does this man's value change by moving from one country to another? No. The perception of his behavior will change, however, depending upon where the action takes place.

Image, again, is fluid and mutable; value and worth are *(or should be)* fixed.

Actions bring results. Engaging in positive action brings positive results. Are you willing to commit to action, though often painful, to achieve the desired result?

Missing Out

Many examples of an attitude of "missing out" come to mind, but the plot below should be recognized by all:

A group of boys, aged 11 to 15 are hanging out at the neighborhood park. Another young man, aged 15, is walking nearby with his girlfriend. This couple is well-attired, with the latest 'gear': expensive team jackets and the current fashion tennis shoes. They seem relaxed and appear to be enjoying their time together. In the next few moments, this couple will be mugged. The group has decided that 'they' don't deserve these nice things, and they take it upon themselves to relieve the pair of these possessions.

Are the members of the group trying to improve their image to the other boys?

Would this be an incident of jealousy?

Notice that in most instances where someone feels they "missed out." someone other than themselves will be blamed, and the individual in that unenviable position will be the target of retribution.

Relate situations where you have "missed out?"

Respect

Respect is status earned over time by appropriate actions. In our Western culture, we have awarded respect to all manner of people based on their perceived image, rather than their actions.

Why?

____
____
____
____
____
____
____
____

Whom do you respect?

____
____
____
____
____
____
____
____
____
____
____

Conclusion

We should be focusing on the only area we have influence to change. How you view yourself, and how you are viewed by others, is image. Image can be changed. Esteem implies value and worth. We are born with value as an intrinsic quality of our humanness. We deserve to be esteemed, cherished, and prized, regardless of image.

The beautiful face or body, the mind of a genius, or Solomon's gold; should not impact one's value – *only their image.* Whether you can be respected has to do with your actions. Your actions mirror character. Respect is the wage earned by your actions. Esteem is an entitlement.

Self-esteem is not a magic pill or panacea, and if you believe it to be, then you're like Clark Kent looking for the phone booth to change into Superman.

If you've avoided people because of a perceived image: height, weight, attractiveness, or intellect… then, shame on you. You may have missed out on connecting with some very valuable people who could have enriched your life. The next time you find yourself awarding time and affection based on image, perhaps you should take stock of your own "cupboard."

Are you ready to make some changes in your life-style? Are you prepared to toss out any erroneous thinking to make the transitions happen? Have you confused your image with your value? Start a new thinking pattern now!

Write a one paragraph statement for change.

May/December?

Is age a factor? How many years older or younger is acceptable? Is chronological age or maturity the deciding factor? Think about this a moment, then write a statement that commits your thoughts.

Should the man be older? What if the woman is older?

What makes age matter?

Chopped Liver

What attributes do you possess that an advertising agency could eulogize to make you a "best seller?" Most marketers do extensive research on their potential market, so that the marketing approach is tailored to the desires of that group. There was a song a few years ago about "looking for love in all the wrong places." Do you have time to engage in such a fruitless endeavor? If not, then, you've got homework to do. List five attributes that make you "marketable". Once you've determined what your merits are, you'll need to think about who your "target" audience is. Involve yourself in the activities of this group. The more time you spend in proximity to like-minded people, the more likely it is that you'll attract a mate.

My Five Marketable Attributes.

Selling Chopped Liver

Where do we begin? I saw some interesting ads in the newspaper. The section was titled "Friendship ads." The requirements were for you to call a 900 number to leave your response to their write-up. I have enclosed some interesting styles. There is usually a charge for this service.

Green Eyed Tigris

SWF, 31, seeks big-hearted jungle cat to romp and play. Must be 31-50, easygoing, and ready to explore life. N/S preferred. 5' 9" or taller a plus.

Nice As Ice

SWF, 35, blue eyed brunette, 5'5", 160 lb., attractive, easygoing, humorous, self-employed with son/daughter, seeks someone similar who is clean cut, financially secure for LTR.

Lots To Give

DWCF, 44, college-educated, outdoorsy, hard-working, friendly, easy to talk to, loves conversation, rural life, country dancing. Seeking upbeat CM, 40-50. N/S, N/D, for friendship possible LTR.

Each one of the above ads is looking for a certain kind of relationship. What can you tell about them?

Write your ad here.

My other ideas to 'Sell Chopped Liver' are.

____

____

____

____

____

3) Temperament

This section is not meant to be a treatise on personality types or temperaments. Rather, it is a few words to the wise. If you are one who thrives on flux and change, then you are probably best suited to another who thrives on this same fluidity. If, however, you are settled and dogged, you would, undoubtedly, find more comfort with one like yourself. Within each group are a vast array of personality and temperament types.

Your own personality and temperament may change with the seasons; your age, sleep patterns, and experiences. I propose that if you stay within your flux or staid group, personalities and temperaments will meld. Keep in mind, though, that we all have fluctuating energy levels. Do not mistake a low energy day for a permanent change in the emotional weather.

Again, flux or staid? After you've figured out where you land, you're better equipped to find a partner. Personality and temperament will be secondary factors, to be surveyed after you've found your personality group.

How long in relationships?

What has been your average time in past relationships? Is that average stated in weeks, months, or years? If all past relationships have been short-term, have you considered why they ended so quickly? Are you the kind of person who, when the going got tough, you get going? Have you been lazy in past relationships, unwilling to commit time or energy? Maybe the reverse is true of you. Maybe you stayed overlong in dead-end relationships.

What would you consider an appropriate time frame in which to decide the future of your relationship? If things haven't moved forward after six months, is it time to call it quits? What about a year or two?

4) Life-style

What is my style?

Are you thoughtful or non-thoughtful? What is your dating style? Most daters could be classed in one camp or the other. The non-thoughtful person takes things as they come; doesn't invest great amounts of forethought in where to go or what to do. Common attitudes result in invitations like: "I'm going to Mickey D's for a burger, wanna come along?" The thoughtful person, on the other hand "creates" dating "experiences." A common date for one of these folks might include a limo, flowers, wine, other gifts, and unusual or expensive dating destinations. The non-thoughtful dater doesn't put a high priority on "dates," whereas the thoughtful dater wants to assure that the dates will become memorable.

Are you a thoughtful dater or a non-thoughtful dater? If, you have scrupulously determined that you are among the non-thoughtful, have you assessed whether this attitude colors other aspects of your life? Take a moment to think about the other life-style habits that influence your dating style. Are you relaxed, reserved, active, passive, sports-minded, inclined to recreate, or do you and your couch share an intimate relationship?

Define your style in fifty words or less. Be candid.

What is my dating attitude?

Bean said "I think I'll go out and circle the herd; see if I can pick off a weak one."

What is Bean's dating attitude? Does this attitude strike you as predatory? Is there an attitude of disrespect here? Does Bean really believe that women are no higher on the food chain than cattle? Do you have any attitudes like this?

Take a few moments to check your dating barometer. Define your dating attitude.

Romantic?

One concept of romance might be just to tell another "I care for you." Someone else may require wine, music, soft lights and endearing conversation.

Small bit of advice; if you are aware of how another person thinks early on in the relationship, do not complain if they do not change to your point of view later.

What do you define as being romantic?

Does "No" mean "Yes?"

Not long ago, a survey of high school boys found a disturbing common thought pattern. When questioned about incidents of "date rape", the survey found that most boys believed there were mitigating factors that excused or absolved the accused. Some of these factors cited by the young men are: that the women were dressing in a manner considered either provocative or inviting; drinking or drug-taking; and accepting an invitation to their residence.

The survey also found that many young men believed that when a lady said 'NO' to a sexual advance that they really meant "Yes." The woman did not know what she wanted and it was up to them to decide for her. Are women communicating their true desires and being misunderstood; are mixed messages being sent, or is there simply an unwillingness to really "hear" one another?

Have you found yourself buying into this thinking? Assess your thoughts here.

If you are a female reading this, you should understand that the responsibility for your protection rests with *you*. When dressing up for a night out, think about how your appearance will be perceived. Watch your behavior so that you are not sending out confusing messages. Above all, take the responsibility to initiate the conversation during a first or second date to discuss the above survey. At an appropriate point, ask your date for their thoughts on the matter. If this conversation leads to discomfort or fear for your safety, it then is your responsibility to leave. Ask to be taken home, call a cab or a friend; *but leave.*

May I Have This Dance?

Most women I know find dancing an enjoyable experience. Many are frustrated, because the men in their lives don't dance, and seem unwilling to learn. Be advised that a man who likes to dance, whether or not he is good at it, will always find women to date. Once it's is known that you dance, women will be asking ***you*** out.

You don't need to be Gene Kelly to learn the waltz, swing, two-step, or the popular line dancing that is in vogue at country music clubs.

Many singles clubs offer inexpensive dance lessons, or the members know where to go to get the best buys.

Now comes the query: what are you going to do about improving your dancing skills?

Junkyard Reject?

You don't need to drive a new car to get a date, but the condition and the cleanliness of your auto will make a difference. If your car looks like it's been used by the crash-test dummies, or it is in serious need of a bath, the dates you'll attract will probably match your car. What date would perceive themselves in a positive light being seen in it?

In many aspects, your auto's condition will be seen as a reflection of you. Go to the information on "image." Is your vehicle a moving trash can? Is this the image you want to project?

Smoking?

If you smoke, you have to know that you can stop. Write down the reasons why you haven't quit.

Respect and attendance

With the advent of feminism, some men have gotten the idea that women are offended when doors are opened, chairs are pulled out, or their meal is ordered for them. Some women prefer to be treated with deference. Most women, however, still recognize such attention as honoring and esteeming their womanhood. So, if you believe that manners and respectful attendance are out-moded, guess again. Nine times out of ten, this attention will be appreciated.

When I date, who opens the door?

Friend

The other day, an acquaintance remarked in conversation, "I thought that he was a friend, but I found all he wanted to do was to party and drink. It was not our friendship that was important, but the drinking."

This conversation prompted me to reevaluate the type of relationships I wanted to have.

Define a friend.

Define an acquaintance.

The friend chart may assist you in assessing where people you know fit. First, go through and just fill in names. Come back and do the further evaluation. This exercise may require some thought. Fun, huh?

Friends Evaluation Form

Name	Friend or Acquaintance	Shared Interests or Activities	What kind of Influence?	Should Relationship Change?
1. Fred *(Sample)*	Acquaintance	Parties and drinking	Enables me to drink	
2.				
3.				
4.				
5.				
6.				
7.				
8.				
9.				

5) Moral Sense

Webster's defines moral as: ethical, noble, principled, or virtuous. This section is not meant to pass judgment on you. Consider it a signpost; whatever your moral sense, a partner of like mind will suit you best. If your conscience is operational, don't waste time with one whose is not. The conscience will become seared by being over-ridden too long with self indulgence.

Rate your moral sense on a scale of 1-10 (one being amoral, ten being obsessively moral). Where do your friends fall on this scale? Acquaintances?

6) I Care

Thoughtfulness is a trait taught through example by our parents and our culture. Some of us have learned the lessons well; some have not.

I am not one to give many gifts. I think we can fall into a trap trying to buy affection. On the other hand, laziness is a factor on my part. Some place a lot of importance on gift-giving; others may not.

It is not always a factor of thoughtlessness, but of family style. This is one of the areas I keep trying to be aware of in my daily living.

I have made a list of times when people show their thoughtfulness. I would ask that you not rate yourself in these situations, but acknowledge that they exist. Develop a strategy.

This is what I will do for a birthday.

This is what I will do for Mother's day.

This is what I will do for Father's day.

This is what I will do for Christmas.

This is what I will do for Valentine's day.

This is what I will do for a child's birth.

This is what I will do on our anniversary.

This is how I will handle spontaneous gift giving.

This is what I will do every day.

Gift-giving should not be of high importance; but for Westerners, it has become a part of our culture. My view is that many women place too much importance on these particular days, when the real message they've been trying to send is that just they want to be remembered.

What if you brought flowers to your lady just because it's the third Tuesday in April? Would she appreciate the gesture, or would it engender some suspicion because you're not the gift giving type?

7) Life Mapping

We have spoken of relationships in terms of roads and road hazards. I would suggest that this analogy can be carried further to encompass the intertwining and connecting of roads as part of a purposeful plan. By first looking at your "map" you may find more pleasant or expedient travel routes. Since most of us plan even a simple vacation, and "map" out where we'd like to go and how we might get there, I propose that we invest equal time and passion in life-mapping. Some suggestions below on how to begin:

1. ***Past:*** I might suggest a paragraph on what you have done. Where you were born and some of your accomplishments. I was born in a small town in Montana.
2. ***Present:*** What are your present living arrangements? Do you rent an apartment? What is your employment? What hobbies do you engage in? What do you do for fun? Who do you spend time with? What are your leisure pleasures? How close are you with family and friends?
3. ***Future:*** I want to do in: one year, two years, three years, retirement, twilight years.

Life Map Planning Form

Present Environment	I want to do	When
Living in Eugene	Live on a sailboat in the south Pacific	In 3 years
?	Graduate from High School	?
Live in an apartment	Buy a home	?
?	?	Retirement

Write a short note of what "Present Environment" you are wanting to change. How you are wanting things to be in the "I want to do" area. When you are finished, set a realistic time to have it accomplished.

Life Map Diagram

Insert below from this partial list; graduate from High School, first job, marriage to _____________, divorce from _____________ child, single, start drugs, stop drugs, military, injury, disease, parent demise, debt free, addressed 'deadlocks from personal growth', gave back to the community, hobby, study, retirement, twilight years, death, 'I want to' _________.

age 20	age 30	age 40	age 50	age 60	age 70	age 80

8) Wants

Stand up and take responsibility for your wanting. Most of your friends will say I need this or that and brush off the responsibility for the desire. You may have heard of the difference but have you ever stopped yourself when you say "I need this," and listen to what you have just said. *Again*, the need is a requirement for staying alive. Will you die without the object or action. I would guess not. Though if it is a need then demand whatever it is to keep yourself alive.

Men Say

This is a list of wants that men say they desire in a female.

Adventure, affectionate, attractive, creative, cuddling, earth-mother, easygoing, emotionally available, financially secure, fit, fun, hand holding, happy, healthy, hedonist, holistic, honest, hugs, intelligent, kids, laughs, no drugs, no kids, no smoking, one man woman, outdoorsy, outgoing, passion, petite, playful, positive attitude, romance, self aware, self confident, self employed, sense of humor, sexy, slender, smoker OK, soul mate, spiritual, spontaneous, vivacious, well educated, well groomed, young mind.

You may add your wants to this list.

What Do I Want?

What do I think are desirable traits? I have listed my wishes alphabetically.

a. Appreciation of others
b. Ability to take her at face value
c. Caring; a person with integrity
d. Has her life under manageable control. The control she uses is that she only "runs her self."
e. Reasonably attractive.
f. Recreational companionship.
g. Sense of humor.
h. Sexual fulfillment.
i. Takes pride in her environment.
j. Wants me.

Picture the woman of your dreams. Can you write it down here?

Date now?

Maybe it would be best to wait for awhile. If you have just left one relationship, another is not the answer. A period of adjustment as a single is necessary. This time period allows us to sort out what happened and how to adjust to the changes.

If you are recently single, there are at least four phases you'll go through before you are in a position to begin healthy dating:

> ***numbness:*** still assessing what happened, disconnectedness, and no desire for a new relationship.
> ***panic:*** not yet adjusted to life without a partner and in too much of a hurry to "be with" someone; anyone.
> ***adapting:*** beginning to appreciate one's own company; finding a partner is no longer *THE* major concern.
> **refocus**: a looking toward healthy relationships; having left the emotional baggage behind.

So; what stage am I in?

Comfort Zone?

I do not think any of us pick a day where dating is going to be comfortable. I believe dating is a skill-based activity. We acquire a comfortable sense through practice. The obvious conclusion is that there is a period of being uncomfortable in developing these skills. Some of us never get beyond the early stages. For myself and many of my male friends, it is uncomfortable to ask a woman out at any time. We practice at it, we take the chance of being turned down.

Where will you practice to acquire this skill?

The Object of Dating

Some of the objectives of dating I hear are: social, sexual fulfillment, sexual excitement, security, another income, fun, friendship, recreational companionship, ego fulfillment, a cure for loneliness, something to do, marriage, a parent for my children.

Do you find your reasons for dating on the foregoing list? What others would you add?

Scattered or Focused

A shotgun dating pattern may keep you moving with nonstop excitement, but there is little substance and no depth. A relationship that is sustainable and healthy requires roots that continually seek greater depth. Depth is not an option in shotgun dating.

Quality or Quantity? What motivated your choice?

Two Peas?

"Two peas in a pod" is more than a cute cliché. Think about it. They aren't just close in proximity, but share the same "home," the same vine, and the same sod. Beyond the similarity of kind, they both require the same "nutrients" to survive and flourish. We're not just talking about any two green orbs; these two "belong" together. Have you been trying to fit a kumquat into your pea pod? Have you been floating along, expecting your "perfect" mate to land on your doorstep, or have you captained a course to succeed in this quest? Remember, first define your objective, then plot a course to that place. What would your "pea" look like? Take a moment to describe the pod-mate.

You can describe your pod-mate here.

Who Pays?

There are many variables: economic levels of each party, who did the asking, attitudes of each person, and the dollar amount in question (a $3 matinee or a cruise). Other factors that may contribute to the decision might be: ego, power, or independence. Perhaps the most workable solution would be that, initially, the one asking should pay.

If the relationship develops, this should be a topic of discussion.

My views are?

____

____

____

____

____

____

____

____

____

____

____

____

____

____

____

Who's asking?

It truly is the female who allows the male courting privileges. Once the female approves, she signals the male. Even with this approval, the male will generally proceed with some trepidation. To proceed with too much vigor could lead to an ear-boxing. We might take a lesson from the wolves, bears, swans, and others in the animal kingdom. The mating rituals are long and arduous; the resultant bonding is usually for life.

So, who asks who? I'm split on the issue. Some surveys point to a longer, more stable relationship when the male initiates the dating process. The time period and locale where you were raised will be a factor in how you see this. Where the relationship is "going" will be a consideration, as well as where you've been.

In our parents' day, men almost exclusively did the pursuing. In today's world, many women and men feel that this should no longer remain the sole domain of men. Women have made inroads to territories which have traditionally been male-dominated. Many roles are reversing and much of the playing field has been leveled. Lest we wax nostalgic, not all things of the past were as glorious as our rose-colored glasses make them out to be.

Bottom line… consider what is most comfortable in the given situation. Listen for clues in conversation that might guide the process. Take a chance and just ask!

Define your comfort zone about who should ask whom and why.

Handicapped?

Many of us would like to think that we respond with kindness to a handicapped person. In assisting someone on an occasional basis, this gives us a sense of helping out and we feel good about ourselves. We are not restricted by their problems twenty-four hours a day. As much as we like to think that this may be the "right thing," the actuality is, it's just darn tough. The difficulty lies in dealing with the situation day-to-day. There is often no relief to the care-giver. Think through with care your feelings of altruism.

Which should rule in this situation, your head or your heart? Why?

You decide — No — You decide

"Where would you like to go tonight?" "Oh, I don't care; you decide." Does this ring your de-ja-vu-bells?

What a hard one. Initially, there is much exploration of interests. The person who asks has a task set for them. A flavor is set for the future by the environment of the first get together. A coffee date at a public restaurant provides safety in a crowd for a "getting-to-know-you" experience. Maybe, if you're the one asking, you should already have some ideas for your date's consideration.

List places that you'd be comfortable taking a person on the first date.

Color Blind?

There was a day when this was not an issue. The majority of the races would not cross over to the other. The biggest tragedy today is the attitudes about the children born of mixed race. Cruelty knows no racial boundaries, and other children reflect their parents' prejudices.

We have our own strong beliefs on this issue. Have you ever written down your prejudices?

My additions to this chapter

Chapter 5

Who Are You?

We spend a lot of time and energy describing and picturing the person of our dreams. Therefore, we focus most of the time on the other, rather than ourselves. Now that we have gone through the sections "Who Am I," and "What Do I Want," let's begin looking for the person you may someday want to call your "Significant Other." This person would have to possess some skills and traits that are desirable. The endeavor is not like fishing where you keep everything over so many inches. I would equate it more to gem hunting or gold panning. You've got to discard a lot of slag. The muscles ache and the days are long in the search of that "keeper," so let's get started. We don't want to make a career out of this... do we?

1.) Relational Skills

Each individual operates within their unique language map. Words have been given meaning by experience. The longer we spend time with another, the more we enter into their language mapping, and the more we understand their word values and interpretations.

Since we are looking for experience and skills, the more relationships a person has had, the more skills you would think that they would possess. The ability to work within a relationship ought to be easier, but it doesn't always work that way. They may get stuck in the groove of incorrect habit. It will take hard work to make changes.

So, how would you critique another to see if they had learned new healthy skills from their last relationship(s)?

____

____

____

____

____

____

Interest in me?

For you to explore what I think or value is a compliment. What people skills did you use to show interest in me? We each use what we think will attract another. What did you do with conversation? Was there just talk about non personal items or did I hear some personal stuff? During the early stages of dating there is a scramble to find common interests. Can the other stop talking long enough to hear me? Does this person consider my interests?

What other benchmarks of showing interest would you add?

____

____

____

____

____

____

How open?

Sure… there are horrible people out there. How guarded should you be? Will you be as open with acquaintances as with friends?

Where do you draw the line on disclosure?

____

____

____

____

____

____

Gather and sort?

Visual? Tactile? Audio? I would ask how a person learns. Do you enjoy body massages? Would you like the person you are with to give these massages? Then I would guess that you are tactile and would appreciate one like yourself.

Why would this make a difference?

____

____

____

____

____

____

____

____

Do you have the time?

"I would have called, been by, written, etc., but I've been so busy. I haven't had the time." If you have made this statement, you know what a smoke screen it is. You have not been sincere. Time can always be found to fulfill a deep desire.

What will you do if someone you are interested in uses this rationale?

Personality?

There has been a lot developed on different personality types. Most colleges or Junior colleges offer courses on this subject. Go take a course. This study is not about defining types but to consider how another will impact you.

Social, artistic, introspective, fun, silly, one brick short, political, caring, etc.?

What type do you get along with best?

Time alone or with other friends?

This can become a control or dependency issue, or a matter of jealousy. If you prefer to enjoy quiet time alone, do not hook up with someone who is very outgoing.

What is the response when I say that I want to spend the evening by myself?

Conflicts in the type of work and work schedule?

Long-haul truck driver, works shift, works nights, works weekends, does not work. This might be as tough as, " when is our normal bedtime?" Is it important to go to bed at the same time? Because of the conflicts in our schedules are we separated for periods of time?

What about the image of the other's employment?

What's so funny?

It is so very easy to go beyond simple innocent humor to making fun of another. We can do horrible damage to another from poking fun. Levity done well relaxes most tense situations. Relationships thrive on clean humor.

Do they have to pull someone aside to tell their joke?

Pleasant?

Do they treat sales people courteously? Would they be a pleasure to be around? When they drive, are other drivers subject to their verbal outrage?

Detail an incident that defines this person as either a blessing or curse to be around.

Advocate?

Most of us are modest. We find telling about our accomplishments, skills and deeds difficult. How pleasant to be with someone who notices enough to promote us. I especially find pleasing one who will defend me when I am not present. This ally shows an interest and concern for me; *what a compliment.*

Which friends support you in this manner?

Caregiver?

Whether or not you have the nurturing "instinct" will become an issue if you or your partner become debilitated in the future. Should you not also consider whether each of you has the capacity to caretake the other should an unforeseen crisis of health occur?

Could you caretake your partner without resentment? Would they caretake you, likewise?

Sorry

"Sorry" is used today, it seems to me, in at least three different fashions. The first is the expression of empathy to another about a problem. "Oh, I'm so sorry you fell and broke your leg." You did not cause the broken leg, but are "Sorry," nonetheless.

The second example is the "first aid fix" apology. The "Sorry" is said quickly to avoid further conflict. It is not usually heartfelt, nor has enough time elapsed that it could be well considered. The hasty apology springs from selfishness rather than a sincere desire to make amends. The third group of people constantly apologize to keep any conflict at bay. If "I'm sorry" will give the situation a quick fix, then it will be said, regardless of whether or not it is sincere.

The major difference between the last two groups is their base motivation. The first quick-fixer is utterly selfish, the latter is most interested in keeping peace, and therefore has a more altruistic motive.

Are you a fixer? Are they?

This is hard work

Every relationship requires hard work from time to time. Day to day, relationships should be fairly easy to maintain.

Does the phrase "I don't want to deal with it" enter their language very often?

Tough times

Depending upon the age of the individual, their prior history in relationships will tell how they weather tough times. The only criteria that I know of is how they operated in the past. The person who believes in long-term relationships, but has had a series of two to three year partners, is fooling who? Conversely, someone coming out of a ten-year relationship has a will to keep things going. Is there a will to keep the relationship going when times get tough?

If problems persist, is there a willingness to seek counsel? What would be a signal that a professional should be considered?

Team player?

Team player is one who asks the question, "What is best for the team," is group minded and solicits group agreement. If the group does not fit, find another group (team) that does.

Have they been in a team relationship before, now, ever?

____

____

____

____

____

____

____

Loner?

Being alone can have its own reward, though isolation to a fault can indicate some psychological issues which should be addressed and resolved.

Is there a healthy mix of time alone and time shared with others? Is their idea of time alone with you simply an extension of their isolation? Is there ever a feeling of being a captive?

____

____

____

____

____

____

____

____

____

____

Birth order?

The personality type is often influenced by where we are in the birth order.

What have you noticed about the three categories of birth-order children?

Oldest?

Second, middle, in-between

Youngest

Exhale?

Can you relax and be yourself? Do you seem to walk on egg shells? Do you sense being at ease in their presence?

Can they relax with you?

Cherish?

Whom do they cherish?

Degree of closeness?

If you do not want someone to touch you as a gesture of friendship or affection, do not be involved with one who has this desire. For one that desires touching, the lack of this contact may produce ill feelings.

Would their definition of closeness include: affectionate touching, hand-holding, kissing?

Social Situations

Have we discussed when to leave a social gathering? Is there a prearranged set of signals to express our desires in a group of people? Am I proud to be out with this person? Do they behave inappropriately in a group?

Evaluate your last social get together...

2.) History

Divorced (single) how long?

There are stages one goes through after a breakup. These documented stages are: denial, disbelief, anger, resentment, and resolution.

At what stage do you want to become involved in another relationship? Are they still struggling with a prior relationship? Why was the prior relationship so devastating? How long has it been since the breakup? Is the progress average for the length of time single?

Background check

Why would I not hire someone to do a check on this person? A background check may be as simple as checking with their friends, to getting a detailed report from a detective firm. Perhaps the best resolution to this is to seek companions who share common acquaintances.

What checking will I do?

____

____

____

____

____

Is this person a predator?

Do not laugh. They are out there. Beware... sometimes they appear as a wonderful person we can't live without. We just have to have a date with that person. "I knew he was a little wild, but I might have made the difference in his life. For me, he would settle down." What a crock. What an exceptional person I am to think that I can make them change. Usually, after getting to know this person, we find that they are a jerk.

Since this is my story, I will use a woman in the next example. What if the next time you received a hug from an acquaintance she lingered. She then makes a pass at you. What if you were in a committed relationship at the time. What of the woman who gave no consideration to the other female? I would call her a predator. A person I would want to avoid.

We all hate to be "taken." So often, looks and mannerisms are so deceiving. Appearance and the manner are often so pleasant. The sad lessons in life are sometimes encounters with these people. It is the kind of person that they are. They do know better.

(A friend once said, "Though I may appear paranoid, it doesn't mean they're not out to get me.")

Who do you know that fits the above? Why?

____

____

____

____

Dumper or Dumpee?

There seems to be more caution to enter into a new relationship by the person that has had their relationship terminated without their consent. Was there discussion by both parties, or did one make the unilateral decision to leave.

Were they dumped? Ever?

On the rebound?

How would they define rebound and have they completed this stage?

Issues?

Did they make a statement similar to this: "I have some issues from my prior relationship I am still working out?" Further questioning may be in order. There may be some major trauma involved that they have not worked through.

What issues? Will you support them as they continue to work through the problems, or must all issues be resolved before you'll consider involvement?

Longevity

Does this person have a stable "job" history? Did the romance last three years, then shortly thereafter the relationship or marriage ended?

What is the job history?

The X?

From having become friends to no contact.

How is it impacting their life now?

Parents?

Have the parents become real people? Do they like being around my parents or theirs? What are the parent styles? Where are the holidays spent, your parents or mine? Maybe we ought to just stay home.

When was the last time you visited? What did you/I do there then?

Children?

Is the concept "my child is perfect" or is it "average children learn and grow by exploring the environment, tempered by a caring parental influence." I have the opinion that a well-behaved child all of the time is one living under constant parental control.

Are children people? When are they accorded that status in your thinking; your partners?

Siblings?

Where does the family get together most of the time? Is there a black sheep? Why?

How important is it to spend time with brothers and sisters? If you met your siblings socially (you did not know them previously), would you find enough common ground to develop friendships? Should we be friends with our siblings?

What is her/his relationship with siblings?

Who is the family leader? How do they impact the dynamics of the family?

Friends?

The ranges seem to be from: Occasional get together, an ear is glued to the phone, friends come first, no friends.

How much time is spent with friends?

What kind of friends?

So what kind of friends do they have? Social, good influence, bad influence, those that have addictive behavior, high places, based on an activity, etc.?

Health problems?

The difficulty of a courtship is tough enough without taking on the burden of a major health issue. Once committed or married, health issues take on a whole different flavor. There is a high possibility that you will be a care-giver of the other at some point in your relationship.

I will ask if there are health problems. Before I ask, I will write my response to the answers I may get.

Aids

Diabetes

Heart Failure

Herpes

MS

Others (you enter type)

3.) Life-style

Life-style?

What are our mutual life-style priorities?

Of He/She individually?

Physical or nonphysical?

Playing cards or working out, or a balance of both?

List their activities:

Physical

Nonphysical

Hygiene

Are we afraid of hurting someone's self image by telling them that they have a body odor (or problem of any type)? Would we be a friend by letting them know of a problem they may not be aware of?

What stinks?

Drugs?

Pot? Sedative? Crack? Has there been counseling for drug usage? Did they ever use drugs? What kind, how much, when and when last?

Drinking?

None, almost never, light, social, in denial of having a problem? Would I date a recovering drinker? Is beer hard liquor? Can a person be a drunk if they only drink beer or wine?

Smoking?

What are their views about smoking?

Tidy or sloppy?

Do they enjoy clutter? Never dust? Wears sloppy dress? Can you "eat off the floor," or are even the dishes off limits? Is there pride in their environment?

Economics?

Are economic levels consistent with one another? We've all heard the fairy tale of Cinderella, but in the real world, rarely do people from divergent economic backgrounds succeed in their relationships. World views are colored by economics as well as experiences. Is she a "material girl?" Is she deeply in debt? Are you?

Romantic?

How do they define "romantic?"

Music?

Are there common areas of appreciation? What styles of music do we both enjoy?

Couch Potato?

It would be difficult for one who would enjoy much physical activity to be involved with one who likes a lot of TV. Maybe the issue is the type of TV programs?

How much TV is watched daily?

4.) Moral Sense

Amoral/Fanatic?

How much time is spent in religious activities?

5.) You Care

Signs of caring

What importance does this person place on anniversaries, birthdays and Christmas? What other signs of caring are displayed-not associated with a special day?

6.) Wants

Women say

This is a list of wants that women say they desire in a mate.

Active life-style, adventurous, artists, attractive, caring, clean companion, compassionate, considerate, country living, cowboy, cries at movies, dark man, devoted, down to earth, dreads, easy going, educated, emotionally secure, energetic, enjoys life, enthusiast, ethics, faithful, family comes first, financially secure, fit, friendship, full of vim & vigor, fun, gentleman, goal oriented, handsome, happy, healthy, honesty, humorous, independent, integrity, intelligent, interesting, kind, likes animals, likes kids, lives healthy, love, loyalty, marriage, masterful, morals, nice looking, no games, no drugs, non judgmental, non smoker, open, passionate, personable, relationship, respect, romance, rugged, self sufficient, self assured, sense of humor sensitive, singing, silly, sincere, single dad, slim, social drinker, short, spontaneous, sweet, tall, thoughtful, trustworthy, well groomed.

You may add to this list.

I think women want

1. Security
2. Companionship and conversation
3. Emotional support
4. The sense of rapport (spark, attraction, in harmony with, whatever words that are used to describe the concept of physical attraction)
5. Sense of humor
6. To be appreciated
7. Affection
8. Love making

Do you think security is number one?

My additions to this chapter

Chapter 6

Activities

This subject has a lot of impact throughout our lives. When we first meet there is an exploration of interests and ideas. What is often done during the early times, cannot be sustained day to day.

I would suggest exploring interests you might do on your own. You are not going to spend twenty four hours a day together. Each person should have their own interests.

The quality and quantity of time spent together deserves a place of higher priority than is usually accorded it. Couples often drift apart due to a lack of time together. If they do not want to spend five hours each night working on cars with you, it would be best to find this out early. If you do not want to spend three hours each day quilting, determine what you would like to be doing instead.

Not all activities ought to be done together. Shared activities, though, facilitate bonding.

Activities for women and men

Antiques, arts shows, baseball, basketball, beaches, biking, bird watching, bowling, camping, candlelight dinners, car races, car shows, church activities, computers, conversation, cooking, time together, country western music, cuddling, dancing, deadheading, dining, doll making and collecting, drumming, football, festivals, fishing, football games, gardening, getaways for the weekend (ski lodge, Reno, Oregon coast, etc.), golf, hiking, history, hunting, juggling, karaoke, laser games, massage, movies, music, new things, old rock, outdoors, parachuting, photography, poetry, pool, quiet times at home, reading, rock climbing, rock hounding, rock music, rodeos, sailing, sail plane rides, shows, shopping, sports, sunrise, sunsets, swimming, tennis, theater, travel, trains, walking, whale watching, whimsy style poetry, wine tasting, and working out.

Define what "fun" means to you?

This would be a good time to ask yourself: "What do I do for fun?"

Ask several women what they like to do. Make a list.

____

____

____

____

____

____

Ask the person you are with what is on their activities list.

____

____

____

____

____

What do you want to do, guys?

____

____

____

____

____

Activities I want to do by myself.

This would include by myself or with other friends.

____

____

____

____

____

____

Activities they want to do by themselves

Did you ask? Just because you are not included does not mean you are not important.

Activities we will do together

The bulk of your list should fall into this group.

My additions to this chapter.

Chapter 7

Discussion Topics

What is a discussion?

A discussion is an exchange between parties meant to enlighten, inform or engage; the purpose is to enhance understanding.

Problems often occurs when the "discussions" are staging areas for the dance of ideas meant to sway another's thinking.

Discussion Ground Rules

Whether you are engaging in general discussion, or attempting to resolve an issue, there are some ground rules both parties must commit to:

1. When you have the "floor," limit your conversation to your own issues.
2. Audit your statements before they exit your lips.

3. Do not engage in name-calling.
4. Do not attempt to place fault or blame.
5 If you are not convinced the other has "heard" you, ask for a paraphrase.
6. When you are satisfied that you have been understood, relinquish the floor, and become an engaged listener.

Ice Breakers

Easing into a discussion you may try some teaser questions. Take turns with the following series of ice breakers.

Describe yourself as a warning label. What does your label read?

____

You are a flower (do not cringe, guys). What variety? Why?

____

You are a novel. What type? (romance, historic, classic, mystery, etc.)

Your vocabulary has been limited to ten words only. List the words.

You have ten minutes with any figure in history. Whom would you choose? Why? Would you talk or listen?

Name five truths that you have learned during your lifetime. When did you learn of them? Discuss what meaning each has for you.

If a machine could be invented to do any task for you that you dislike, what would it do?

For twenty four hours you can 'switch" with someone (you can be them, and they can be you). You will each have access to all the other has, including thoughts, memories, emotions, and desires. With whom would you trade places?

Background

Widow or Widower?

Is there a realization that there is, nor ever was, a perfect marriage? It may be difficult for the remaining spouse not to idealize a former relationship. There may be a tendency to compare only the good memories of before. We cannot compete with someone who is deceased. We should not have to.

How will I respond to excessive nostalgia?

____

____

____

____

____

____

What would you say about your X?

You receive a phone call asking about your X. The person inquires about some details of what went on. Now they are involved and have become concerned about an issue.

Would you answer their queries? Why?

____

____

____

____

____

____

____

____

____

____

____

____

Children

Corporal Punishment?

Will hitting or spanking be permitted? Is anger a permissible part of discipline? Who will be responsible for discipline? Does the person assuming the responsibility have the perseverance to follow through with appropriate action to facilitate compliance? If you ground them, restrict activities, etc., will you have to be there to enforce the punishment?

Who will do the disciplining, or will it be shared?

Favoritism?

It takes a lot of work not to play favorites. The cliché that blood is thicker than water is usually true.

What ideas do you have to create an atmosphere of equality?

Common front?

Though partners may disagree on specific issues, prudent parents will realize that they must appear as a united front. Children recognize early to pit one parent against another. It is not uncommon, either, when a new adult enters the picture, for children to create wedges and instigate crises. You should both resolve early to never disagree in the presence of children, unless you are prepared to have it used as ammunition against you.

Children may be told or intuit that there is disagreement, but should know that the bottom line is that a common ground will be found, and the adult disagreement will be resolved by the adults. Children must understand that they do not have the power to make or change the rules.

Who's on First?

Many dilemmas are created because there is a struggle for position within a "family" unit. Some individuals believe that their partner will always hold the position of priority over children. What is far more reasonable is to realize that the situation itself should determine the priorities, based upon what ultimately benefits the entire unit.

If, for example, Mary Ellen wants to play tennis on Saturday, but Jimmie has his first Little League game, which should assume priority?

If Bob was offered a new job on the East Coast at twice his current income, but the children don't want to move because they'll miss their friends, which decision ultimately benefits the unit? See where we're going on this?

Make your ideas concrete. Write them here.

____

____

____

____

More children

Pregnancy? Adoption? Insemination? Children by a former deceased husband? At this juncture you may be saying, "Wahoo, wait a minute... deceased husband? With the advent of artificial insemination and sperm banks, this isn't as absurd as it sounds. There are some potential moral and ethical questions that must be addressed.

If pregnancy is opted for, will there be discussion about where and how the birthing takes place? Will the partner be in attendance? Does the woman want him there? These are important issues which deserve consideration.

What if one partner wants more children, and the other doesn't? How will you resolve the impasse? Is the relationship worth resolving such disagreements? Would moving on to another relationship be more prudent?

Articulate your ideas now.

Willing to accept someone else's children?

If only one of the partners has children, is the other willing to accept those children? If there is unwillingness, is it resolvable; or, should the relationship be reconsidered?

Issues of Closeness

Affection

Anyone who was raised in an environment of affection will find it uncomfortable to partner with one who avoids affection like they avoid disease. Correspondingly, the non-affectionate person will be uncomfortable with a partner who is naturally affectionate. Determine early on your respective affection barometers, and decide if you can live with any differences you find. The chances of changing either type personality are slim at best.

What do you deem to be gestures of affection?

Long-term relationships?

Are you truly interested? Perhaps if you've been single ten or more years, you have passively decided not to enter into a long-term commitment. Taking no action is still a decision.

How long have you been single? Why?

Exclusive?

At what point would the relationship become exclusive? When would it be appropriate to cease dating others and commit to monogamy?

Are you able to be monogamous? This is a valid question. If either partner is perpetually "in heat," will monogamy be too restrictive?

If "variety" is not the spice of life, write down your idiom of choice.

Complacency

We are not talking here about that stage of all relationships where some of the volatility has simmered down, or the passion has waned. We are talking about more of an attitude toward the other partner that includes many things: laziness, ambivalence, taking for granted, lack of caring, inattentiveness, etc. There is some dissatisfaction with the status quo, yet an unwillingness, or inability, to change. Partners in this pattern look more like roommates than lovers. There has been a shift from considering the two as one to an attitude of "every man for himself."

List three creative ideas you have to keep complacency at bay.

Health & Recreation

Aids test?

Should both you and a potential partner take a blood test for AIDS, HIV, and STD's, to alleviate fear of any possible life-threatening illnesses?

Should this topic be covered when you discuss sexual histories?

Before sex

There are some topics that should be discussed before engaging in a sexual relationship. The type and scope of the relationship will dictate which of the topics are most appropriate to discuss. Should you talk about marriage, past or future sexual history, condom usage, or health issues?

List three topics you think should be discussed prior to sex...

____

____

____

____

____

____

Do we talk about suicide?

If, in the course of learning about the other person's history, you hear allusions to suicide, or they themselves have considered suicide as a remedy for an "untenable" situation, perhaps discussion in this area is warranted. Then, you can determine if the issue has been dealt with in a healthy way, or there is a real call for psychological intervention.

List the facts you know about suicide: i.e., age range, symptoms, contributing factors, gender propensity, etc...

____

____

____

____

____

____

____

____

____

Vacation?

If you think about it, vacations start as one person's idea. There seems to be a process of convincing or of "selling the idea." Is the sale consummated when the other party is convinced that there is a potential for enjoyment? If the other person agrees to go, what then? Will they make their partner miserable or resentful if they do not enjoy themselves? If one agrees to go along, then it becomes their responsibility to create their own enjoyment.

Should vacations always be taken together, or are there times when being separated serves the relationship better? If the couple does not get along well fifty-one weeks of the year, will one week of vacation make much difference? If separate vacations are chosen, is it done to avoid spending time alone together?

Define vacation?

Is a vacation a time to enjoy each other or the event?

Can a compromise work? Maybe this year do your thing, and next, your partner's? Could one vacation encompass events both parties would enjoy?

Formal

Traditionally, a vacation is a pre-planned event, taken as a unit, to a destination away from home and work. Because these are often planned months or years in advance, are usually costly, and involve being away for longer than a weekend, potential for problems is higher. On the "up" side, there is a chance to make the planning process part of a memorable vacation.

Informal

The informal getaway is generally more impromptu. Agreement is more forthcoming. The spontaneous vacation will often involve a day or two, rather than the week or longer "formal" vacation.

Vacation activities?

List your three choices

List their three choices

Health Benefits

With a significant portion of the population not covered by an insurance plan, the potential for disaster is horrendous. One stay in the hospital can be a financial catastrophe for most people. One may be burdened with so much debt that their quality of life will continue to decline for the remainder of their life.

What health coverage is available?

Retirement Benefits?

At some point we all reach the stage when, by choice or by circumstance, we must retire. If that seems like a far distant horizon, guess again. The older you get, the more quickly the years pass, and the only certifiable method of avoidance is death.

Lest that stage catch you completely unprepared, now is a good time to begin your plan. What dreams would you like to fulfill during those years? Have you considered how they are to be realized?

Outline your plan:

Money

Do you think money is power? Why?

What is your definition of pocket money? How should pocket money be spent?

How involved will each partner be in spending decisions?

Will only one person handle the finances?

How many check books are there to be? Who will keep track of them physically? What access does the other person have to the check books?

Is there child support? Spousal support?

Has either person accumulated a large debt? What is the nature of the debt?

Will you take on their financial burden? Will they take on your financial burden?

What credit cards are carried and by whom?

How much (credit) debt may one person incur without the approval of the other?

What are your "feelings" about money?

What are your "ideas" about money?

Employment?

How involved will each of you be in the other's job? Do you both have an understanding of what your partner's jobs entail? Without this knowledge, can you be compassionate when your partner has had a bad day? Can you be an effective sounding board?

Is employment just a job? How will their employment impact me? Would I be expected to attend social gatherings? Would I be expected to donate my time to their firm (employer)? What expectations do our employers have for us?

Paycheck or partner?

Being conscientious about one's job is not a detriment, but an obsession with work is. Do either of you volunteer to work longer than is necessary, choosing to be absent from the relationship as a result? If your employer expects you to work late every evening and on weekends, and it interferes with time rightly committed to your partner, what takes priority? Who owns your heart?

Combine households?

There are as many reasons to combine household: to save money; to be together more; to take steps towards marriage, or, to have to caretake, etc. Below are some questions to ponder ***before*** you make any plans to combine worlds.

Do we move in to one or the other's home, or find a new one together? Who decides what gets kept, and what gets tossed? Who decides whose stuff goes where? What happens if there is a breakup later? How easy is it to remember all of your stuff, my stuff, and our stuff? Does the person moving in have an area all their own? Did you commit the conversation about combining households to memory or is something written down more desirable? Write down your thoughts here:

What will the effect be on the one moving in? Is there a sense that the house is "our home?"

What will the effect be on the person whose home is being moved into? Does the other party have to get permission to make changes in decorating? Will putting children's pictures on display be a bother?

Pets

Animals come with responsibilities. When we have our own pets we can keep up with fleas and ticks and other problems. Now we are involved with another person and their pets. What if their dog has worms? What if they will not take the pet to the vet for deworming?

My pet?

How many is enough, and what kind of animals are they? Why would I sleep in bed with a pet? Do I expect my partner to sleep with my pet(s)?

Their pet?

Will I accept your pet? Am I expected to walk your dog (cat, rat, mouse, etc.)? If your dog jumps up on me will I discipline it? I do not allow pets in the house, but what about you?

Politics & Religion

Is formal religion important?

What do you want to talk about: attending services, teaching, becoming a pastor, going to church only on Sunday, etc.?

Is politics important

Do you view politics as power? Will there be active involvement in political issues? What issues require more than just a discussion?

Issues of Integrity

Secrets?

How vulnerable and candid should we be? Openness may be the best policy, but sometimes the premium is exorbitant. Perhaps not all the details are necessary. Also consider the motivation for airing all the dirty linen.

Example: past prison time, extramarital affair(s), abuse, difficulty controlling anger, gambling? Again; are there hidden debts? Would I ask to see a credit report? How about a motor vehicle report?

Which areas of a person's past must be shared, and which things should be withheld?

Issues of Privacy

Are there subjects that cannot be discussed? How do you decide when and how much to be vulnerable? Can you ever feel safe?

What's off limits?

Photos, diary, purse, wallet, tools, my stuff, your stuff. Is it necessary? Have we discussed this issue and come to some agreements? Write your thoughts.

What are the boundaries?

Let's talk about whether there are boundaries to include personal space, time, etc.?

Write your definition of relationship boundaries.

Respect

Due Respect

How do we show an appropriate degree of politeness and respect toward one another? Are we owed respect or is it earned?

Inappropriate displays of anger?

Anger can be a way to control another person. Most anger is rooted in fear. There is a fear of loss, either material or emotional. Is angry communication a habit in our relationship?

Why do you become angry? Write about the last time you were angry and the trigger(s) for the anger.

Does physical violence play a part?

I love her, but she hits me all of the time... Should I hit her back? What do you do about physical violence?

Taking Responsibility

What is incorrect about these statements?

"Men and women have different needs." "He or she does not fill my needs." "I need this."

I would guess that this person has several problems. The emphasis is on the outcome rather than on taking responsibility for the want.

What else do you think is going on?

What didn't we do in prior relationships that may have prevented the breakup?

Example: I could have initiated getting back together sooner after an argument. I always made (them) apologize to me. In spite of the fact that it will be hard, I will make an effort to be the one to end the argument.

Was there a factor that could have made a difference?

What will prevent this relationship from going the way the others have gone?

"If you don't work it out in this relationship, you will have to work it out in the next."

If prior relationships ended badly, what do I do about this one to make it different?

How willing are we to discuss and take responsibility for past mistakes? What were the past mistakes? (Is this enough room, or too much)?

Was there marriage counseling in a prior relationship?

Who initiated it? Who stopped going? How long did they go? Were they willing to resolve difficulties when times got tough? Well, why did you go?

Expectations

Are they too high or too low? Should there be expectations? Since we are in the discussion portion of this study, what expectations do you want to bring up? Will these be expectations of the other, of the relationship, or of yourself?

You can put your ideas here.

Who does what?

Discuss each task: housework, maintenance, yard work, cooking, etc.? Will you work at tasks as a team, or will there be specific jobs each takes on regularly?

Are there gender-specific jobs?

What tasks do you do?

What tasks do I do?

What tasks do we do together?

World View

Dreams?

One of mine is that someday I will sail my boat out of Portland, Oregon and head for Mexico for an extended stay.

What are your dreams? Are you willing to make any sacrifices to realize these dreams? List them.

What means a lot to her or him?

What things can I be flexible in and what areas shall I make no concessions.

One of my beliefs is that I take people at face value. Are they believable? A statement was made to me, "I do not date married men while they are in the process of a divorce." Then that person proceeds to seek involvement with me while I am processing my divorce. This behavior made me unable to take them at face value. I make no concession here.

Did we discuss what means a lot to me? To you? What?

My additions to this chapter

Chapter 8

Non Committed Relational Situations

The Date

A date is two individuals who, by agreement, willingly spend time together. This communing could be a walk, meeting for coffee, bike riding, drive in the country, etc.

Where to meet someone

The easiest way to meet another seems to be in a group of friends or group of people in some organized activity. This can range from a single's club to attending a college course. The object is to be active with a group.

When was the last time you met someone new staying home? We have the task, then, of choosing the type of group that we'd be comfortable with. There are many places to meet someone: newspaper ads, the library, singles club, bar, or hobby clubs.

Relationships that begin with introduction by a mutual friend seem to have smoother starts. There is an implied approval when an introduction is made by a mutual acquaintance.

Take advantage of your networks. We all have them… family, co-workers, civic clubs, business associates, friends, etc. Take a moment and list your networks. Now list in each network at least one person whom you know that you will be comfortable enough to ask about possible introductions. Sound too scary? If you never risk, you might as well *stop right here*… all the workbooks in the world won't move you from your comfortable spot.

Networks available to me and the name of a contact person.

Network	***Name of contact***
Work	
Church	
Friends	

The asking

Most people make plans for a weekend three to four days ahead. If the event is of some importance, or requires more than a few hours, even more forethought should be given. So, if you're asking, make sure to give yourself and the other party plenty of time. Spontaneity is a worthwhile adventure for later, but for the first couple of times, ask far in advance. Allow the other person time to adjust their schedule, and give them adequate notice of any changes in plans or cancellation. A non-conventional thought would be to send a confirmation note of the upcoming event.

How do you ask? Here are some sagacious suggestions:

There's a new Greek Restaurant opening this Saturday...

I have tickets to...

I would like to go out with you. What do you think?

Do you like...?

I noticed that you have an interest in... I appreciate someone with this interest...I am going to do... I like...You game for...?

What about the shy man or woman who you ***know*** wants to go out, but just can't bring themselves to ask? If you know that they regularly engage in a particular activity, how about inviting yourself along? If it's a guy who fishes, gold pans, likes football or basketball, or is a baseball fan, see if you might tag along on one of these outings.

How would you ask to be included in someone else's plans without being intrusive? Detail a creative scenario.

____

____

____

____

What if she says no?

You notice someone. Their image comes to mind again and again. Then you start to envision what it would be like to be with that person. Next, comes the thought, "I wonder how I could go out with them." Now you start to plot. This is serious business. We run several scenarios through and hit upon a plan. "I heard them talk about ... I will find out when the next... is going on and invite them to go with me."

"How horrible. I asked and they said no. *Is there something wrong with me?* (Remember not to think right or wrong judgments). This is not a nice thing. They should have said yes."

Come on, guys, get a grip; you know who I mean: those who will not take *no* for an answer. What are you doing? If you pestered her and she finally consented, how much pleasure would you derive from going out with her? You would consider her weak and easily manipulated. The less pressure, usually the more enjoyable the experience. If I get turned down, I most often find that there was something going on that I did not see. In the long run, I'm better off.

Do you expect to always get a "yes" answer? How will you respond when you get "no?"

Rejection

The thought finally struck me, after many evenings alone, that I was finding reasons to reject all potential partners. What I determined was that I had some pretty unreasonable expectations. If, for instance, I consider myself a 7 on a scale of 1-10, where did I get the idea that I needed to "save" myself for a female 9 or 10? Have you had this experience? Are you setting your standard so high that failure is assured?

Why would you sabotage yourself in this way? What is really going on? Are there other issues at play here? Does fear play some role?

Getting ready

I like lists. The written word requires me to add emphasis to the task at hand. When it is important it is helpful to have this aid. The following is a partial listing of the preparation for a date.

1. Car clean and gassed up
2. Tickets.
3. Reservations.
4. Flowers, gift.
5 Grooming; clothes, shoes, hair, and bathed.
6. Mental note of ideas or topics to discuss.
7. Recheck your calendar for time and date.
8. Check map for address.
9. What else are you to do?

____

____

____

____

____

____

Stood up

At 5:00p.m. the phone rang. I answered, She said, "I'm sorry I can't meet you at 6:00p.m. for our date. I don't feel well." She went on to explain, "I was out with a girlfriend last night and we stayed out too late. Today I ran errands, and haven't had time to rest. I feel like I'm coming down with something." She was very apologetic and professed that she wanted to go out with me.

That next weekend I had a date with a different woman. After picking her up she said to me, " I stayed home last night. I wanted to make sure that I was rested for our date. This is important to me." What a *difference* and what a *wonderful* evening we had.

Were you ever stood up? What can you surmise from what happened?

First date

The first impression makes such a difference. The first time out of the chute I go just to have a good time. I leave the set of questions elsewhere. I try not to be overcautious in my discussions. I try to concentrate on whether I'm enjoying myself and the other person.

What is your first date agenda?

Second date

Now I start to subtly probe and question. Well, maybe not so subtle. Time is a factor. I evaluate if I want to continue to spend my time based on these factors: possible friendship, serious relationship, or "this is not going anywhere."

What do you evaluate?

Third date

I must be serious about this potential friend, or there is the possibility of a long term relationship.

Friend or relationship?

The next day

Call her, send flowers, send a note. Your depth of involvement here will tell her how much interest there is on your part.

What displays of appreciation are you comfortable with?

____

____

____

____

____

____

____

____

How dates are discussed

Do we describe without thinking about what we are saying? Dates are discussed differently depending on what you are looking for. The descriptions vary by age and sex. What did you say the last time you told of an encounter with another?

Situation:

> ***She:*** "I went out with this really neat Doctor."
> ***He:*** "I went out with this really cute blond."

Interpretation:

> ***She:*** "I want security. Maybe I can stay home and do the leisure things I have always wanted to do. As a Doctor's wife, I will have security and not have to worry about money."
> ***He:*** "I want a fulfilling sex life. An attractive mate is important to me. I only want to go out with beautiful, slim women. With that woman in my possession, I would be the envy of the guys."

Situation:

She: "Really buff, but bad, he has a cute butt, the chemistry was there; we talked a lot; he has personality. What an exciting night."
He: "I scored with this wild chick; she knew what to do."

Interpretation:

She: "Visually he appeals to me. He is naughty but nice. I like his appearance. He turns me on. We could talk about what is important to me. I want fun and activity with this person who takes the initiative."
He: "Sex is the most important thing to me. Everything else is second."

Situation:

She: "I met someone who I had a wonderful time with. We got along so well."
He: "I think I met the woman of my dreams."

Interpretation:

She: You fill in the thought here.

____

____

____

____

____

He: You fill in the thought here.

____

____

____

____

My sense of the other is?

Our senses take into consideration all of our evaluation processes. Women often call it intuition. Pay attention. Your feelings, mind, physical, and spiritual self is seldom incorrect when all are taken into consideration.

What is your "gut" reaction?

____

____

____

____

____

____

Evaluation of the date

What contraindication was there that this would be a good relationship?

The things in common are nice but, look for a major obstacle. These are the encumbrances that will sabotage the relationship. They are the big ones: child abuse, alcoholism, batterer, drug abuse, disabled, major health problem, prison time, etc.

Does anything stand out?

____

____

____

____

____

____

____

____

____

____

My intention with this person is?

Whether we state it consciously, we always develop an intention with a person. Much of the time we do not sort through enough to clearly define where we are going. Stop and visualize what the relationship can become.

Is this what you want?

You sure are nice... You smell good, too.

There is a period of time in the evaluation when we are not quite sure of how much we want to get involved. We are definitely interested but don't want to say the "C" word. We want to spend time with the other, but… we want a few more non-committed dates.

How am I going to structure communicating my intention?

Setting the Environment

Let's look at this from the perspective of you as the driver of a vehicle, approaching the freeway. Are you so aloof that you're nearly stalled at the on ramp? Are you the casual sightseer, content to follow the flow of traffic, or do you tend toward the frenetic, passing all other traffic so you can be the leader? Your "driving style" often sets the tone of your relationships.

Have you considered the comfort of your passengers? How does your "driving" affect them?

Breaking up

A breakup begins with a thought. An idea creeps into the mind. You alone choose what value and power the thought warrants. If you nurture it, feed, and stimulate it, the idea has the power to sustain itself. You, however, may elect to terminate the power of any thought by refusing to fuel it. Some thoughts need reassessment, some require positive action; some annihilation.

You will require a great deal of emotional energy to endure a breakup. Where will you derive that power? You can gain power from anger, fear, confusion, resentment, and bitterness, or from a reasoned, settled, logical and mature outlook. Restated, you can do it with a great deal of emotional upheaval or be calmly logical.

What to do

If you're thinking of ending a relationship, you should first do some serious thinking. Make a list of what you believe are the reasons you want to terminate the relationship. Maybe one of your reasons looks something like: "She's let herself go; she's gained weight, and always looks like a slob." In a space next to these "reasons" get candid with yourself and state the ***real*** reason. "I'm embarrassed to be seen with her." Once all of your real reasons are solidified in your mind, you'll possess the power to communicate them without creating smoke-screens or using anger to fuel the breakup.

What not to do

Don't expect good advice from friends or family. They have a history with you to protect, and may not be operating at 'face value' with you. If you want to discuss the relationship with someone, pay for counseling. Sharing relationship woes and secrets with anyone else can lead to misery down the road.

What is done

Many people who break off a relationship have someone else in the wings. There is either the idea of someone who appears attractive to them, or they are involved with someone. The old "greener grass" theory is alive and well.

Most find a reason to blame the other for the breakup. The statements proposed sound silly when examined in the light.

> **"I need some space."**
> "I want us to be friends, but I need some space." I would interpret this as: "I want to be able to call upon you while I transition out of this relationship. You can make it easier for me by being available.

When I find someone, then I won't call you when I am lonely or wanting to go out when no one else is available."

"I don't love you any more."

"You were attractive and convenient when we got together, but now I want something different. I do not know what but ..." *Stop... Whoa...* Well who is out there that appears more attractive now? It seems like an examination of your definition of love is called for.

"You've changed." (smoke screen)

"I will not take the responsibility for the breakup; guess I will put the blame on you."

"I've outgrown John." (smoke screen)

I have decided to breakup this relationship. This is a way that I can avoid a real reason.

What reasons have you given and why?

Gossip *(it gets around)*

Invariably, what goes around, comes back to haunt. We should act as though all of our conversations are being monitored. In truth, most times they are. The incentive to keep a secret other than your own is minimal. So, remember, anything you say, can and probably will be used against you.

Moral outrage

Even if you are outraged beyond reason, the divulging of secrets or sharing of information with the sole motive of bringing hurt, harm, or embarrassment to another is not acceptable. Rise above the temptation to be this petty.

My additions to this chapter

Chapter 9

The Big C *(commitment)*

This can be a wonderful time in a relationship. Both can be who they are to the other to the fullest extent. A rapport may be established that allows sharing and communication in a safe environment. Trust has been established and vulnerability is shared.

The agreement;

Building A Solid Foundation

One of the beauties of being a couple is to be able to say, "We believe in." There is such a basis of understanding between us that we can almost speak for the other. (I would not suggest that you do this). I would suggest a written agreement. It would define what the basis is for the relationship. Most of the agreements would be in broad terms, certain areas would benefit from specific language.

Sample Agreement

We, ______________________________ and ______________________________ agree that the following are some fully understood premises for our relationship. We have discussed them, they are us.

A. I will take my partner at face value.
B. Our foundation will be built on teamwork.
C. The goal is to cherish each other all the days of our lives.
D. There will be no power bases apart from this one.
E. The relationship shall be exclusive to each other.
F. Sex is a mutually enjoyed commitment. Either may say no upon occasion.
G. The difficulties of the relationship shall remain within the relationship. We will work out our problems together.
H. Money
    1. Each shall contribute to the household account. The amount that we each shall contribute will be based on [(50%) or (proportionate share of income.)or(?)] (You enter the agreeded upon share here)
    2. (Enter name) shall handle the household account.
    3. No party shall spend more than ($200) of the household money without a discussion with the other.
    4. Each party will maintain their own personal account. If an amount is to be spent exceeds $1,000.00, they will check in with the other and advise them of the spending. Yearly, each agrees to disclose balances of their personal accounts to the other.
    5. No credit purchases shall be made over $100.00, without *permission* of the other.
I. No changes to this agreement shall be make without a full discussion and they shall be committed to writing.

Add to the agreement to fit your own situation.

____

____

Prenuptial

Opinions vary on this one. Some state, "If we need it, then something is wrong." Or, "Each situation is different."

What of the person who has a house going in, and wants to keep it if there is a divorce in five years. The agreement could be set up so that in ten years everything is shared, and a split would be an equal division for both parties.

When marriage is clearly the intent, the following prenuptial could be of some consideration:

1. All property which belongs to each prior to marriage shall remain in their personal estate
2. After marriage, each party shall have the full right to manage their property as each would have if they were not married.
3. In the event of separation or divorce, the parties shall have no claim or division of property acquired prior to marriage.
4. In the event of separation or divorce, the property acquired after marriage shall become subject to equal division.
5. After ten years of a continuous marriage, it is deemed that all property has been a commingled, that assets and property are jointly owned.
6. In the event of death, each party's estate passes to the other

The above is not intended as legal advice. Check with your attorney for the laws of your state.

What would you add to the agreement?

____

____

____

____

____

____

My additions to this chapter

Conclusion

We often do not credit ourselves with the effort we invest or in the hard work that we do. This is about what makes relationships work. If you have waded through this material you deserve extensive credit.

You know the routine; don't just sit there. Picture yourself getting patted on the back. Reflect on what a task you've accomplished. You did a great job! Congratulations!

Index

About the author;

Wayne Marsonette is a mid-fifties single father. He spent a total of thirty-one years in two marriages and has two young adult daughters. He is the owner of a medical equipment and foster placement company in Springfield, Oregon, where his employees will tell you he's a pretty decent guy, even though they prefer it when he goes sailing.

Please Send Additional Copies of

Potholes, *Speed* Bumps & Long Dusty Roads

Send To Name ______________________________

My Name ______________________________

Address ______________________________

City ______________________________

State ____________________ ZIP __________

Phone (   ) ______________________________

Please send a check or money order for $12.95 for each book. Shipping and Handling is $3.50 for the first book and $1.00 for each additional copy.

Mail to:

GeminImage Publishing

PO Box 70712

Eugene, Or 97401

FAX (541) 744-7122

You may copy this form for additional orders.